# YOUR WEDDING

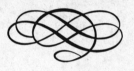

# YOUR WEDDING

## A COMPLETE GUIDE TO PLANNING AND ENJOYING IT

## NANCY PICCIONE

Prentice-Hall, Inc.
Englewood Cliffs, New Jersey 07632

*Your Wedding: A Complete Guide to Planning and Enjoying It*
by Nancy Piccione
Copyright © 1982 by Nancy Piccione

Printed in the United States of America
Prentice-Hall International, Inc., London/Prentice-Hall of Australia, Pty. Ltd.,
Sydney/Prentice-Hall of Canada, Ltd., Toronto/Prentice-Hall of India Private
Ltd., New Delhi/Prentice-Hall of Japan, Inc., Tokyo/Prentice-Hall of Southeast
Asia Pte. Ltd., Singapore/Whitehall Books Limited, Wellington, New Zealand
10 9 8 7 6 5

Library of Congress Cataloging in Publication Data
Piccione, Nancy.
Your wedding.
Includes index.
1. Weddings. 2. Wedding etiquette. I. Title.
HQ745.P49     395'.22     81–15681
AACR2


ISBN 0-13-981407-8 {PBK}
ISBN 0-13-981415-9

# A DEDICATION

The people at Alfred Angelo have been in the bridal business longer than anyone. They've watched trends come and go, traditions fade away and reappear, fashion popularity rise and wane. Through it all, they've seen one tendency remain constant: Wedding dresses are unique garments, happy by the very cause of their existence. Just like the Piccione family.

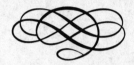

# CONTENTS

# INTRODUCTION

This book is for everyone who is planning a wedding but isn't quite sure how to do it. It's also for everyone who is planning a wedding and is sure of what they want. Because once you've chosen what you want, you'll need to decide how best to get it.

The format of the book is dedicated to the proposition that a wedding, by its very definition, should be a celebration, a time of sharing, a solemn and official act that takes place in an atmosphere of happiness. Any happy celebration that is shared with close friends and relatives should not be difficult to achieve. Rather, it should be pleasurable and, if not extremely simple, at least logical—like A, B, C. Our alphabet proceeds with order but provides an infinite choice of words. And your wedding should be like this. Any possible combination of mood, style, taste, and comfort should be within your reach. What's needed is the plan, the order of events that will provide for the combination.

Tradition has done well for us. But we've come to a time, in our society and in our own lives, when we have a deeper appreciation of what tradition represents, and a greater understanding of the fact that, just because etiquette is the given, we need not be bound up in it. For tradition should connote graciousness. Etiquette means the security of participating in an act that has been tried, tested, and approved. And we've learned that there are other acts that have not been tested that *will* be approved if they are planned with taste and executed with consideration and respect for anyone who will be even remotely involved. After all, tradition began somewhere. Someone was first.

And your wedding is a first. The occasion will arise only once, the moment of its realization will happen only at the precise time and in the singular manner that you so choose. There is no right or wrong way to plan your wedding. There's only what will make you happy, in the traditional sense, in these contemporary times.

This book will be different from others you've seen on the subject because its goal is to be concise, easy to read—not hard to look up a particular item you need to know about. Most of all, this book is meant to be enjoyable, just like your wedding. Facts and fun. You'll be surprised at how much you already know, how much you sense correctly. We are creatures of comfort, and any rule that overemphasizes propriety and infringes on the ease we wish to share with people close to us, in a party atmosphere, will not sit well with our indicators of common sense, our interpretation of kindness and good cheer. And everyone's interpretation is different, so we've gone full circle. There is more than one way to celebrate a wedding, and it's your choice.

The book will not quote prices, because our wonderful world of modern technology provides us with the grand opportunity of comparison shopping; it is fact that you can plan a wedding for as much or as little as you are able to spend. Of course, the kind of wedding will be determined by your budget, but the actual marriage can take place in a variety of circumstances, expensive or inexpensive. Besides, today's prices are about as reliable as the weather. They change constantly.

The "you" of this book is you, the bride. The "you and your" of the book is the bride and the groom. For it is the couple that will be doing the marrying and therefore should have the wedding they want. If one statement is repeated over and over, it is that you and your groom should do whatever you wish when planning your wedding, as long as you do it with the good taste that led you to make a commitment to each other in the first place.

Some things will never be out of date. Consider moonlight and love songs. They are ageless because they are important to our own well-being. Weddings will never be out of date.

# 1
# ANNOUNCEMENTS

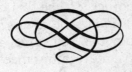

*Annabelle: It says here that we need to send all of our vital statistics to the newspaper three weeks in advance, have a huge party, then Dad breaks the news with the first big toast. . . .*

*Albert: Here, honey, step right out here on the balcony with me. OK, now, we'll take care of this ourselves. Ready . . . one, two, three . . .*

*Both: (loudly) WE'RE GETTING MARRIED!*

Next to the actual wedding itself, announcing your engagement is probably one of the most fun events of getting married. It elicits the most spontaneous response from family and friends, expressions of joy and happiness for you and your spouse-to-be. The reactions can range from the gleeful surprise of a younger relative to the "I knew it was just a matter of time" reply from your dearest confidante.

Your parents—all four, yours and your groom's —should be the first people to learn of your good news. Traditionally, the groom's parents would call on the parents of the bride, the mother of the groom writing or telephoning the mother of the bride. However, today many brides do not live in the towns in which they grew up; often the groom has relocated as well. Therefore, arrangements to have the families meet should be made as soon as possible. Once you have notified your parents, dear relatives and friends should be informed by telephone or personal note. You wouldn't want those people who are closest to you to read about your engagement in the newspaper. You may choose to visit each family separately to share the news. If your parents are divorced, it is wise to tell each of them yourself that you plan to marry, and do so as simultaneously as possible. As you begin to speak of the details of your relationship, the plans for your wedding and the celebration to follow, and how you arrived at the happy decision to wed, remember that not all parents or relatives of an older generation will want to be informed of intimacies surrounding your personal lives together. So even if you and your husband-to-be have been living together for a long period of time, take into account the feelings of those who would be sensitive to this type of discussion.

If you choose to wear an engagement ring, do so immediately. The average engagement period today is four to ten months, although it may be shorter or as long as a year. This time is usually devoted to planning your wedding, and if your parents are going to make a formal announcement, they should schedule this with the length of the engagement period in mind. Six months is the average amount of time required to plan a formal wedding. More time than this may make for an engagement period that becomes too drawn out, unless distance or personal matters demand additional time.

Formal newspaper announcements of your engagement are usually made in the locale where you and your fiancé reside and in the towns where each set of parents lives. Check each newspaper for their exact requirements and deadlines; ask your future mother-in-law to do this for her local paper if your fiancé's family lives far away. If you see an engagement announcement that you particularly like, clip it and use it for a guide. Some papers supply a standard form for you to complete. As you make your announcement, remember the basic rule of journalism, the four *W*'s: Answer the questions *who, what, where,* and *when.* Your announcement should be typed, double-spaced, on one side of an 8½- by 11-inch sheet of paper. In the upper right-hand corner of the first page you should include your name, address, and telephone number, or that of a person in the vicinity of the journal's circulation who could verify all of the information and answer any questions that an editor might have. Also include a release date at the top of the announcement; the newspaper is not permitted to print the information prior to that date. If you have had your engagement party and are prepared to make your engagement known to the general public, simply include the phrase "For immediate release, please" at the top of your announcement sheet. It is ideal timing if the newspaper announcement can appear the day after the engagement party. Give all newspapers the same release date and fresh—not carbon—copies of the information. Provide accurate and precise details. Do not use nicknames unless a full name would be totally unrecognizable, and check the spelling of names thrice over. The academic achievements of the bride and groom and the positions they now hold may be mentioned. When a student has not graduated from a particular school, the term *attended* is used. At the end of your announcement include the date, time, and place of the wedding, if you so desire. If you haven't scheduled the specifics, a general phrase such as "A spring wedding is planned" should be used. All announcements are written in third person, just as if you were telling a story about other people. Remember, you need to supply only that information you care to announce publicly.

Your parents usually make the announcement, although there are varying situations. If one of your parents is deceased, the announcement may read:

> *The engagement of Miss Mary Theresa Miller,*
> *daughter of Mr. James Miller and the late Mrs. Miller,*
> *to Mr. Walter Johnson,*
> *son of Mr. and Mrs. Stanley Johnson*
> *is announced by the bride's father.*

If your parents are divorced, the announcement is made by the parent with whom you live or lived, but both parents are mentioned. If both divorced parents wish to announce the engagement, they may do so by including their names separately, and the announcement would read:

> *Mr. James Pearlman and Mrs. (or Ms.) Audrey Pearlman*
> *(or Mrs. Vincent Nelson or Mrs. or Ms. Audrey Nelson,*
> *if she has remarried)*
> *announce the engagement of their daughter Harriet,*
> *to John Sparks, son of Mr. and Mrs. William Sparks*
> *of Philadelphia, Pennsylvania.*

If the paper will print a photograph and you would like to include one, either of yourself or of you and your husband-to-be, it should be an eight- by ten-inch glossy. Check with the editor; sometimes a five- by seven-inch photo is acceptable. Any photograph submitted to a publication should include a typed caption of identification on a separate piece of paper, which should be taped on the reverse of the photo. Do not write directly on the back of the photograph. In mailing or hand delivering photographs, a piece of stiff cardboard the same size as the photo should be included in the envelope so the picture is not creased, bent, or folded in any way. Do check that the photograph stands a good chance of being printed before you send one to the newspaper. Some journals will not return used or unused photos unless this is specifically arranged. Any announcements or photographs should be mailed to the newspaper with a return address, first class.

Many newspapers, especially those in larger metropolitan areas, will print either your engagement announcement or your wedding announcement, but will not publish both. Decide which printing is more valuable and meaningful to you, your groom, and your families. In the case of a second wedding, when a bride is divorced and marrying again, she usually would not announce her engagement formally, but would announce her wedding.

A very formal wedding announcement would be sent in press-release form to the society page of the newspaper approximately three weeks in advance of the wedding. It would include the bride's maiden name; the groom's name; and the hour, place, and date of the ceremony. This date would determine the actual release date of the information, although it is wise to have the specific date you wish the information to be published clearly designated at the top of the sheet. The officiator's name and the names of the members of the wedding party and their relationship to the bride and groom are listed next. This is followed by a description of the bride's and bridesmaids' dresses and flowers, and the place where the reception was held  The names and occupations of the parents of the bride and the parents of the groom are included next, as well as the academic credits and employment of both the bride and groom. This type of formal, detailed article usually concludes with the announcement of where the couple will live after their marriage.

Remember that an announcement of engagement is optional for all brides, and if you so choose, you may simply dispense with the formal announcement of engagement and proceed directly to the sending of invitations to your wedding.

# 2
# BRIDAL WEAR—
# ATTIRE FOR THE
# WEDDING PARTY

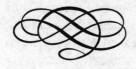

*Bunny: Purple is the most regal color; it just screams out elegance. I'd really like to wear a purple wedding dress.*

*Baxter: Sweetheart, you know how partial I am to green, it makes me feel close to the earth. I really think the hunter green tuxedo is the one for me. . . .*

*Both: (after a pause) How about stripes?*

Fashion trends may come and go, but there will always be captivating, enchanting clothing available for weddings. A bridal gown and a tuxedo are theatrical in their effect— regal costumes that produce a very special event. A cotton smock and an Indian shirt and trousers may be a less formal look, but will still prove tasteful if they conform with the mood you wish your wedding to have. Wedding dresses are designed for every type of wedding and every degree of formality. The expert designer is aware that the bride of today comes in many shapes and sizes, lives in a variety of locales, may be very young or much older, and might wish to spend a small or large amount on her wedding ensemble. Specialists in menswear are finding the same variety of characteristics in their customers. And this variety, being the spice of life, means that a bride and groom have options in the clothes they will wear for their wedding that are unprecedented. The most exciting fact about all of this is that a very traditional wedding dress might be accessorized with a very contemporary floral bow; a brand-new jersey fabric might be combined with an ornate imported lace; and a classic bouffant skirt can have the look of yesterday or tomorrow. Today, a bride wears a traditional veil not because she must, but because she looks beautiful in it and it complements her dress. A groom wears a tuxedo because he wishes to be distinguished from the crowd and opts to coordinate his attire with a group of people whom he has chosen to attend him, not because someone told him that he had to do it. Wedding wear can be the single most thrilling visual element of your wedding day; it will make you feel as wonderful on the inside as you appear on the outside. Your attire and that of your wedding party will be visible throughout the entire day, crowning you in glory and symbolizing great celebration. Although the world of fashion is at your command, there are some factors that will always be taken into account—when to start shopping, who chooses what, and which items must be included to achieve the look that is desired. The effect of your appearance will be spectacular, whether you wear a cathedral-length train or a street-length dress with a lace overskirt. The same is true for all your attendants and the members of your family. Shop, sample, try on, experiment with color swatches, consult the fashion experts, read magazines. Do this for your gown, your groom's suit, and your attendants' attire. After all is said and done, choose what makes you feel not just beautiful, but gorgeous!

If you decide to wear a traditional wedding gown, start to shop six months in advance of your wedding date, if possible. You must allow a minimum of three months from the time you place your order at the bridal shop or department store to the time it will arrive from the manufacturer for your fitting. Two more additional weeks will be needed to have the alterations completed. A wedding gown may be the only dress you will ever own that will be custom-fitted to you, made to order— something that the average American who is ensconced in the world of ready-to-wear may not realize. The fact that this garment will be fitted to you and only you is considered a luxury to many, but for such an important dress, it is almost a necessity. Since a wedding gown is a one time garment for the majority of women, you have no expertise or practice in the purchasing of one. However, you do know what feels good, you probably have an excellent sense of what looks good, and you and your groom will have chosen the kind of wedding you want and the degree of formality you wish to achieve. Therefore, you have a certain amount of vital information to take with you when you start to shop for your wedding ensemble. There are experts in the field—sales personnel and bridal consultants who are not only versed in the world of fashion, but are specialists in the fabrics, patterns, and laces of which wedding gowns are made. Seek their advice if you need it, but remember that you—not they—will wear the gown and celebrate the marriage. When you go to a bridal salon, you will see samples that are not just there to look at. Try them on, and remember that many formal, floor-length gowns are cut larger than street wear, so you may need to try a smaller size than you wear every day. Even if you've never worn a ruffle in your life, until you try on the garment with the fully ruffled skirt, you have no idea how it will look on you. You just might like it.

Bridal gowns, like most couture fashion, are designed for two seasons no matter what price range they fall into. The spring/summer collection and the fall/winter collection do vary in fabric and cut, but there are many wedding dresses that are styled to be worn at any time of year. A formal wedding gown is traditionally a full-length white or ivory dress, but many pastel colors for spring and deep-toned velvets for winter are now available. Informal wedding dresses may be white and floor-length, but the veil and train are often omitted. This custom has held true regardless of whether the wedding is held during the day or in the evening. Sleeve length, veil length, and train length vary. Obviously, these choices now become yours.

When you start shopping, take with you shoes with the heel height you will want to wear. (Think ahead to the fact that you'll wear the shoes for a number of hours on your wedding day.) Also, take the underthings that you will need. If you wish to wear an heirloom veil, or if you are shopping for a veil to match an heirloom dress, take the item with you to match color. Talk to your salesperson about every single item, from special undergarment requirements to pins for the headpiece. Remember that gloves, trains, and veils are all optional, but they may be options that will complete your outfit perfectly.

Once you make your decision and place your order, do not schedule your final fitting too far in advance of your actual wedding date. You may gain or lose weight as you cope with what may become an endless stream of activity during the month before your wedding; if you are starting to take the birth-control pill, any doctor will agree that a weight change is very likely.

When your alterations are complete and you take your wedding gown home, hang it on a door in a room that is not trafficked heavily. Take a sheet or a piece of tissue paper and spread the train out completely, so the dress will not wrinkle. Most bridal shops will store the gown until very close to the final hour, so schedule the pickup with this in mind. Ask for pressing instructions for the particular fabric of which your dress is made, just in case of any emergency. Most wedding dresses are pressed with steam on the wrong side, but each garment varies. Your veil may need a touch-up just before you put it on; a warm iron and a delicate touch should be all you need, but ask for instructions for the veil as well. Many people cover the car floor in which the bride travels to the ceremony and the reception with a sheet to keep the dress as clean as possible. Be cautious as you walk steps and enter doorways, and don't be embarrassed to ask for assistance. History states that many medieval women had serving ladies all day long!

If a family member exerts pressure on you to wear an heirloom dress, you might consider this phrase of diplomacy: Say that you have always dreamed of having a wedding dress that is yours alone, and that your dream included all of the details down to the buttons. However, if you do wear an heirloom dress, or any form of antique garment, have it custom-fitted to your measurements, and examine the fabric, seams, and detail work for any extreme wear or damage. If you decide that a bridal gown is not for you, that you would prefer to wear a suit or a semiformal dress, make sure it will be appropriate for the time of day and the type of wedding you plan. You can find this type of garment in the bridal salon. Some of the most elegant dresses in today's bridal collections are designed specifically for the nontraditional look. They include the street-length dress, the bridal suit, and the remarriage dress, all of which can be worn for many other occasions after the wedding. A pretty dress or a suit of soft fabric is usually more in keeping with the celebration than street clothes. You may opt to wear a garment that is traditional to the nationality of your family; it still needs to be fitted to you, and every detail should be approved by an older member of the family or a person who understands the look and can advise you on shoes, headpiece, and flowers that are customarily worn to achieve the proper look.

The final touch to a traditional wedding dress is the wedding veil, or headpiece, or veil with headpiece, or hat, or mantilla, or juliet cap, or picture hat, or floral wreath. More wonderful choices for the bride! A wedding veil should match the color of your dress exactly, and this is easily achieved by purchasing both at the same time and at the same place. If you wish to have a special headpiece made, your bridal shop may be able to order an extra yard of the fabric or lace that your gown is made from. Veils come in many different lengths, and the longest are the most formal. This has far more to do with proportion than tradition; a cathedral-length veil (which may be four yards long) would not look correct with a street-length dress. You will see the variety of veils available to you. Try them on for comfort as well as appearance. You'll find chapel length (three yards), fingertip length, elbow length, straight veils, pyramid veils, tiered and ruffled veils, and an even greater variety of caps and hairbands to which the veil may be attached. When you put the veil on, stand, sit, kneel, bend, turn your head. If dancing will be a major activity at your reception, consider ordering a veil that snaps off the headpiece, or feel free to remove your headpiece entirely after the ceremony. If your wedding is informal, or if you will be married at home, you may choose to wear nothing on your head. A single flower or a full headpiece designed and fitted to you by your florist is another option. Wedding hats that are designed to specifically coordinate with certain styles of full-length wedding gowns are a beautiful look; they may or may not include a short veil or netting. Small earrings and perhaps a string of pearls or an elegant gold chain complete your outfit; very little jewelry need be worn.

After you have selected your dress, or at least have a general idea about what you will wear, you choose your attendants' dresses. The length of the dresses should be the same as yours, and the style should complement what you will wear. Attendants will accept your choice, but take their height and weight, their hairstyles, their coloring, and their budgets into account, for each one is responsible for the purchase of her own dress, shoes, headpiece, if any, and accessories.

Bridesmaids usually all wear the same color and style of dress. However, if you choose to have a "rainbow" wedding, each attendant's dress would be a different color, but identical in style. The maid of honor's dress may vary in style from the other bridesmaids; or you might choose to have her wear the same style, but a different color than the bridesmaids. All of your attendants should wear the same shoes, and if this means dyeing them to match the dress color, make sure that they are all taken care of by the same shoemaker so the colors match perfectly. Their headpieces should match as well; you might opt for flowers for your maids' hair, which solves the problem of choosing a headpiece that must be worn with a variety of hairstyles. Your attendants should wear very little jewelry, small earrings or rings only, and if you would like them to wear an identical item of jewelry, you might make that their thank-you gift. If your attendants are coming from out of town, send them a list with all of the measurement and size requirements the store will need to alter their dresses. However, the final fitting should be scheduled in advance of the wedding day, even if this means arranging for a seamstress to come in and do hems the night before the wedding. You can also send an attendant her dress and have her take care of any necessary alterations in her hometown before she travels to yours. You can order and pay for the dresses and then have each of your attendants reimburse you when they arrive for the wedding. There are certain situations in which the bride's family pays for the bridesmaids' dresses; this option is yours, and the dress itself could be your gift to the attendant—although you will probably wish to get a memento that is somewhat more personal. These are women you know well, and all your decisions should be based on these friendships. Even if you are having a small wedding and will only have one attendant, your maid of honor, your dresses should still be checked to make sure they will blend well together.

Accessories for the bride and the bridesmaids can be many or few. Everyone needs shoes, unless you are being married on the beach. Shoes imply stockings; they should be a neutral color for your attendants, and you may wear a light color, or off-white, never opaque white. Purchase the shoes with enough advance time to break them in, and on the actual wedding day the soles may be scraped on stones or cement to avoid slipping. You might even wish to wear your shoes to the rehearsal. Gloves are not mandatory, even if your dress is short-sleeved. They can be very awkward at the moment when you will exchange rings, so if you would rather not deal with that situation, eliminate the wearing of gloves completely. If, however, you wish to wear gloves to complete your ensemble, you may hand them to your maid of honor at the beginning of the ceremony, or you may cut the stitching of the finger on which you will wear your ring so that the ring may be slipped on without removing the glove. Short or long gloves may be used; long ones are quietly disappearing from the fashion scene. Other accessories include prayer books, parasols, crinolines, garters, handkerchiefs, money bags. Decide what you need, what you must have, then immediately decide what you want, what you would like to have. By combining these two factors you will create a wedding ensemble that is totally comfortable and correct for you and your bridesmaids. Remember to appoint a trusted friend or relative to guard your purse and the handbags of your attendants during the ceremony and, if needed, during the reception. This should be a person who won't mind being at your beck and call with combs and lipsticks for last minute touch-ups, someone who is familiar with where you will dress and where you will all wait for the ceremony to begin. Valuables may also be kept in securely locked cars during the ceremony.

The other ladies of the day will be the mother of the bride and the mother of the groom. Traditionally, the mother of the bride, who was hosting the wedding with her husband, would inform the mother of the groom what length she would wear and what color she would wear. The mother of the groom would then wear the same length and would have to choose another color. These days, as well as the day of the "mother of the bride" dress, have faded away, and now the mothers need not concern themselves with dressing in a similar fashion. They need not—but may—wear the color that the bridesmaids will wear. They will probably want to consult with each other about what each has chosen, but as long as each dresses appropriately, there should be no problem. There is no rule saying that they must wear a headpiece of any sort. The only real issue is the degree of formality, for it is just as incorrect to overdress as to appear too casual. This holds true for anyone who attends any social function.

Your guests will know what attire is appropriate from the invitation you extend to them. If they don't, hopefully they will contact you and ask. If the wedding is very formal and held during evening hours, you may wish to request that all of your guests wear formal attire. The woman who is invited to a number of these social events need not worry if she wears an evening dress more than once. A good dress, classically designed, will defy time limits and remain in fashion for a long duration. There are no restrictions on color for a guest's attire; black may be worn in great taste by anyone but the bridal party. Some of the most glamorous dresses in the world of fashion are designed in beautiful black fabrics. Contrary to former belief, they suggest celebration and can be worn to many an opulent festivity. The only white dress that should not be worn to a wedding is a guest's own wedding gown.

Menswear for weddings is usually rented, and you and your groom should decide what you would like the ushers to wear so orders may be placed six to twelve weeks prior to the wedding date. When you go to a tuxedo shop, take swatches of your bridesmaids' dress fabric if you wish to coordinate a color of outfit rather than opting for a black tuxedo or gray morning suit. There has been a trend toward a combination of menswear at weddings; your groom may wish to be dressed a bit differently than his groomsmen—he might decide to wear a tailcoat or different accessories than his ushers. This trend seems to be due to the fact that today the groom wishes to be distinguished from his ushers in the same way that a bride is distinguished from her attendants. You might decide on any of these options, or you may go the traditional route of having the attendants and the fathers of the bride and groom wear the same outfit that the groom wears. The father of the groom should dress formally if he will stand in the receiving line. Some fathers of brides and grooms are more comfortable in the traditional black tuxedo; they may wear this outfit if they would not feel proper in a more contemporary suit that is chosen for the groomsmen. Fathers usually dress alike, even if they wear a different fashion than the other men. Your advisor should be the expert at the formal-wear rental shop; menswear offers a smaller range of choice than women's, although there will be decisions to be made. Though some people consider a tuxedo a uniform, it is certainly one in which any man, no matter what shape or size, looks extremely handsome if fitted properly. There are a number of tuxedo rental chains that will provide you with measurement cards in mail-order form to send to ushers who will come from a distance; many of these chains will do measurements at one branch and arrange for actual pickup close to the wedding location. Let your merchant know all of your decisions—style, color, and number needed—and have each groomsman stop by for a fitting if possible. Men's suit sizes are fairly standard, but hems will need to be sewn and minor alterations may be necessary. Don't forget any essentials. Shirts should be purchased or rented at the same shop; shoes are the responsibility of each man—they are most often black, although there are some manufacturers who offer color-coordinated shoes to go with the tuxedo. Although the men all pay their own tuxedo rental fee, and the best man usually picks up and returns all of the clothing, the groom pays for ties or ascots and accessories. Handkerchiefs are not worn with a boutonniere, and the ushers do usually wear a flower on their jacket's left lapel. The groom and his best man may wear accessories and boutonnieres (a rose rather than a carnation) that differ from the ushers.

The formality of the menswear is coordinated with and determined by the bridal dress. If the bride will not wear the traditional long dress, train, and veil, the groom may wear a business or a three-piece suit. If the bride wears a street-length suit or dress, the groom may choose a dress blazer and trousers. If the groom decides on a suit, all the accoutrements—white shirt, tie, and vest, if desired—should be chosen with care to present a complete look, rather than a look that will be too casual. The time of year will determine color and fabric—white or khaki may be perfectly fine for summer; a dark fabric should be chosen for winter. Yet another choice for the groom is to coordinate his attire with the period of design of the bridal gown. If the bride wears a beautiful Victorian dress with all the matching accessories of that era, the groom may wish to wear a velvet suit with a ruffled shirt that is reminiscent of the same century. The look you choose for your wedding may transport you to a very special world for one special day, and you are entitled to an extremely elaborate celebration if you so desire. Just make sure that everyone is going in the same direction!

Aside from wedding attire for the actual day of the wedding, it was considered tradition for the bride to assemble a trousseau. This was a collection of clothing that the bride would use for her new life away from the home where she had lived. It often meant that the woman was leaving, for the first time, the house where she grew up, to go to a strange and new living situation with her new master, her husband. Those days are completely gone and most brides have a full wardrobe that they have accumulated over school and college years, and often over time spent pursuing an active business career. If you would like to treat yourself to a few new things, go right ahead, but no one will expect you to change your entire wardrobe or even your basic appearance just because you've changed your marital status.

After your wedding is over, you will have to make a decision about what to do with your wedding gown. It is probably the only one-time garment that will be hanging in your closet, and there are many options open to you. Certain dry-cleaning establishments offer a special treatment and packaging for the gown that will make it easy to store at home. This is not the normal dry-cleaning procedure, but a method designed specifically for garments with intricate beading, delicate lace, and the like. Look in your phone book under Bridal Preservation Services, or ask the salesperson where you purchased your dress to supply you with the name of a company the store recommends highly. The heirlooming process allows you to keep the gown for posterity; you may find that years from now you will have a daughter who would like to try it on, or a relative who has always wanted to be married in an heirloom dress. Many people keep their wedding gowns until they have children and have the gown made into a christening dress for the baptismal ceremony.

Your wedding clothing is something you will remember forever; it will be one of the outstanding features of your wedding photograph album, second only to the people wearing it! Take the time to shop carefully; if you will wear something that you already own, allow for cleaning and alterations. Allow ample time for all of the necessary alterations and adjustments when delivery dates are set for the attire of the wedding party. You will find a wide price range available to you for both your wedding gown and your groom's suit, so do not feel limited by budgetary restrictions. Your clothing should not only look good, it should feel good; so make sure your seamstress and tailor are experts in the art of fitting. As with every element of your wedding, your choice of attire will reflect your good taste.

Everyone is different in appearance, and this is never more evident than in the selection of what people wear. Bridal clothing is one of the most personal decisions you will make. Choose carefully, but with a sense of confidence in your judgment and that of the experts who will assist you, and with a feeling of adventure to try something that will be as unique as your wedding day.

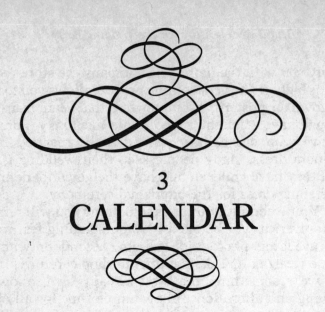

# 3
# CALENDAR

*Carolina: Six months before our wedding, I'll be in India wrapping up the biggest sari contract our company has ever made.*

*Clarence: Six weeks before our wedding, I'll be on a special mission to Alaska to firm up the solar-energy-in-igloos deal.*

*Both: (determinedly) Let's plan the wedding this year and get married next!*

Rather than stating all of the prenuptial necessities in long, descriptive sentences, the calendar following includes key words and phrases. They are intended to provide a concise listing of things to do and when to do them. Each item is elaborated upon in the chapter of its name, so feel free to fold down page corners, underline, circle, or highlight anything that you wish to look up in greater detail. Use the calendar for a checkoff list as your wedding approaches.

Remember that time is your greatest asset and your greatest enemy. By planning ahead, you've taken the risk out of achieving factors essential to your wedding. By letting things go, you may not be able to acquire an important element that you wanted. This holds true regardless of how much time you have; what's far more vital is how well you use the time you do have.

So, whether you have six months (the average amount of time it takes to plan a formal wedding) or six weeks (it has been done!), here are the primary wedding requisites in their typical chronological order. Adapt the list to your needs, allow a little leeway for the unexpected, and start checking off the items you've already completed!

### Six Months Ahead

*Choose the kind of wedding, date, and time.*
*Determine the budget and who will pay for what.*
*Make the guest list.*
*Reserve the wedding and reception locations.*
*Make arrangements with the officiator.*
*Select a color scheme for wedding and reception.*
*Order wedding dress and accessories.*
*Order bridesmaids' attire.*
*List selections with gift registries.*
*Plan where your new home will be.*
*Decide on engagement rings.*
*Make honeymoon plans.*
*Arrange for time off from work, if necessary.*

### Three Months Ahead

*Complete guest list.*
*Order men's attire.*
*Make list for announcements, if necessary.*
*Order invitations.*
*Order stationery.*
*Coordinate mothers' dresses and fathers' attire.*
*Confirm delivery of all attire.*
*Make honeymoon reservations.*
*Engage photographer.*
*Schedule portrait.*
*Have physical examinations and blood tests; decide on birth-control method, if desired.*
*Contact florist.*
*Plan the ceremony.*
*Plan all reception details, from menus to master of ceremonies.*
*Plan music.*

### One Month Ahead

*Mail invitations so they will arrive three weeks before the wedding.*
*Order wedding cake.*
*Have final dress fitting for bride and bridesmaids.*
*Confirm all men's attire orders.*
*Purchase attendants' gifts.*
*Order wedding rings (check the engraving).*
*Plan housing for out-of-town guests.*
*Make reservation for bridesmaids' luncheon.*
*Make arrangements for the rehearsal dinner.*
*Choose wedding presents for each other.*
*Confirm the flower order, bride's bouquet to boutonnieres.*

*Arrange health and life insurance changes, making each other the new beneficiary.*

## Two Weeks Ahead

*Get marriage license.*

*Write and deliver newspaper announcement of marriage to editor.*

*Arrange for transportation to ceremony, reception, and honeymoon getaway for you and the entire wedding party.*

*Make a list of photographs you know you will want taken.*

*Decide on your wedding hairstyle and have your hair done now, in case you decide to change.*

*Make name changes, if any—bank and charge accounts to driver's license.*

*Plan the bachelor party.*

*Reconfirm the honeymoon reservations.*

*Hear the music for the ceremony.*

## One Week Ahead

*Pack for the honeymoon.*

*Address and stamp announcements.*

*Give caterer final estimate of guests who will attend reception.*

*Make seating arrangements, if any, for reception.*

*Brief the head usher on any special seating arrangements for the ceremony.*

*Bridesmaid's luncheon takes place.*

*Bachelor dinner takes place.*

*Give gifts to attendants.*

*Make appointments for facial, manicure, pedicure, hairstylist, barber.*

*Move personal belongings and gifts to new home.*
*Prepare officiator's fee.*

## CONSTANTLY

*Add to or subtract from the calendar list above if your wedding so requires.*

*Write thank-you notes as soon as each gift arrives.*

*Make appointments to meet, in person, anyone you will hire to render services for your wedding, and get all agreements in writing.*

*Consider ideas for home furnishings and personal wardrobe items you'll both want after the wedding.*

*Maintain your sense of humor. Everything listed here should be fun. It's the step-by-step accomplishment of the kind of wedding you and your groom have wanted and planned.*

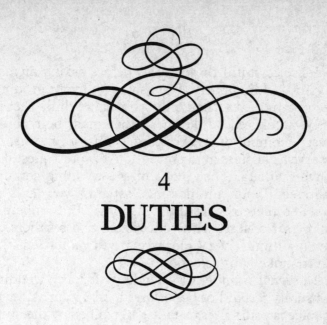

# 4
# DUTIES

*Dolores: Who's responsible for taking the dog to the kennel the day before the wedding?*

*Dagwood: Who's in charge of picking up Great-aunt Bertha at the airport the night before the rehearsal dinner?*

*Both: Darling, there's just one more thing I'd like you to do. . . .*

Although friends and relations you choose as your wedding attendants are close and dear to you, remember that each position implies special duties, so let your practical side show for a moment and consider each person's ability and desire to fulfill these duties before asking anyone to join your wedding party. Just as you and your groom will have certain tasks that only you can fulfill, there are chores—albeit enjoyable ones—that must be completed by every member of the wedding, from your mother, who will serve as hostess at the reception, to your tiniest flower girl, who will take her place in the wedding ceremony. Definitively, your attendants "attend" you and your groom and thereby accept the responsibilities inherent in their roles. So, start with your sisters and brothers, your groom's siblings, very close relatives and friends, and begin to make your selection.

The least number of attendants for any wedding is two, usually a maid of honor and a best man. After that, the choice is yours; it is usually determined by the number of guests invited to the wedding. There should be one usher for every fifty guests, and it is perfectly acceptable to have more ushers than bridesmaids, unless it is important to you that they walk as partners in the recessional. Although it sounds simplistic, your ushers' primary duty is to seat your wedding guests, and this can become a task of major proportion if you are having a large wedding. The ushers offer their right arm to all of the female guests, whether they are accompanied by a man or not. It is helpful if the gentleman you choose to serve as head usher is able to recognize a majority of the guests; therefore, your groom's best buddy from college, who has never met any member of either family, is not the likely candidate for the task. He may certainly be a groomsman, but should not be burdened with the responsibilities of acting as head usher. This is a good example of thinking ahead to practicality in designating your attendants. The ushers will pull the aisle runner into position and pull it back at the end of the ceremony. The ushers remove pew ribbons as the church fills, and at the conclusion of the ceremony they may return to escort out the parents of both bride and groom. They also direct the rest of the guests to exit by standing before the aisle that is to move out. The ushers usually assemble one hour prior to the ceremony; obviously, they should be present from the time of the very first guest's arrival. Just before the ceremony begins, the head usher escorts the bride's mother to her pew, unless the bride's mother's son is a member of the party. In this case, he would accompany his mother down the aisle. The final duty of the ushers is to be available for any small tasks that might pop up at the reception. This might include providing transportation to the reception for the bridesmaids. It is quite nice if each usher dances with the bride and every bridesmaid.

The duties fulfilled by the bridesmaid are those of lending support and assistance in whatever way necessary to the bride, and to be a vital part of the beautiful, decorative picture of happiness that the bridal party creates in celebration of the occasion. They should also mingle with guests and aid the bride and her mother by keeping an eye out for everyone's comfort and relaxation at the reception. Bridesmaids are usually close in age to the bride, and are often relatives of the bride or groom. A junior bridesmaid is between the ages of nine and sixteen. She is often a relative of the bride or groom, and her duties are essentially the same as the bridesmaids. Bridesmaids may take turns standing in the receiving line; junior bridesmaids and ushers do not stand in the receiving line.

The flower girl and ring bearer usually assume the duty of being enchanting and endearing without even knowing it! The ring bearer, usually a child four to seven years old, may be either a boy or girl. It is safest to have the ring bearer carry a substitute ring, but if you choose to entrust your wedding bands to the little one, make sure that they are securely sewn or fastened to the pillow. However, remember that when it comes time for the exchange of rings during the ceremony, the honor attendants should be able to present the rings without delay; this might not be possible if the actual rings are sewn to the pillow. The flower girl is usually four to eight years of age. Both the flower girl and the ring bearer should be chosen for their poise and their ability to participate in a well-behaved manner.

The maid of honor is your personal attendant, and she may be distinguished from the bridesmaids by a slightly different touch in the style or color of her dress and flowers. If the person you choose is married, she is called a matron of honor. You may decide to have both a maid and matron of honor, but you must decide from the start who will serve you during the actual ceremony. The one who will attend you at the altar will follow the other in the processional and will sign your marriage certificate as legal witness to the event. The maid of honor will hold your bouquet during the ceremony, and the groom's ring will be in her safekeeping. She will move your veil at the beginning of the ceremony and adjust your train for the recessional. The maid of honor stands in the receiving line and helps you change into your going-away outfit. Traditionally, she usually hosts a shower in your honor.

The best man is often a brother of the groom or a very close friend; sometimes the groom's father will serve in this capacity, although this is rare. The best man is invaluable to the groom on his wedding day; his duties are many. He accompanies the groom to the ceremony after helping him dress, he carries the wedding ring and the marriage license, he pays the minister, and he checks that the ushers are dressed properly and are sure of their duties. He holds the groom's gloves as he waits for the bride's approach to the chancel steps. The best man proposes the first toast at the reception and reads aloud any telegrams that have arrived. He may take charge of the car keys, tickets, and luggage for the couple's getaway to their honeymoon. He sees to it that all rental clothing of the groom and his ushers is picked up and returned to the rental shop.

From the time your attendants accept your invitation to serve as a member of the bridal party, treat them as a very special part of the entire event. They and their spouses do receive invitations to the wedding and other parties that will be planned. Needless to say, they receive invitations to the rehearsal dinner; they must be present at the rehearsal, as they compose your entire processional and serve as important witnesses to the ceremony. The only exception to the rule of inviting the entire bridal party to any and all of the events is in the case of showers. If you are being showered with showers—if there are a great number of them—let your attendants know that they need not feel obliged to send gifts to all of them. In fact, it is a considerate bride who arranges that each attendant is only invited to one or two of these parties and is informed that a small token or no gift at all is perfectly satisfactory.

The parents of the bride have many duties, due to the fact that they are usually the official host and hostess of the wedding and reception. The mother of the bride is the first person to be greeted in the receiving line and the most important person to thank at the end of the reception. After she is seated at the actual ceremony, no other guests enter, and her presence in the church signals the beginning of the wedding. The bride's father usually escorts his daughter to the church and down the aisle. He is a member of the wedding party, dressing in the same fashion as the groomsmen. He is often included in the receiving line (although this is not mandatory), and he dances the second dance with the bride.

The parents of the groom are honored guests at the

wedding. They are seated just before the mother of the bride is at the ceremony. The mother of the groom stands in the receiving line.

There are myriad details involved in a wedding and reception, and the bigger the affair, the greater number of details you will have to tend to. It is sometimes quite valuable to enlist the help of a few persons who are not official members of the wedding party to handle specific matters. This person or persons may handle the guest book, give signals to the caterer, or direct guests to tables. If you delegate such tasks, make sure to give a gift or memento of thanks. Do remember, though, that too many cooks spoil the stew; your mother, as official hostess (or whoever is officially sponsoring the reception), should remain in command of the situation.

If you so desire, the services of a bridal consultant can be engaged. This person usually takes over completely and does absolutely everything. A bridal consultant will plan the entire reception and all details of your wedding right down to helping you select your dress. He or she will be the authority on all of the duties and obligations you should expect of your attendants as well as all of the service personnel you hire. The consultant will oversee your bridal registry and will be a part of your wedding planning from beginning to end. Bridal consultants are usually located in department stores or bridal salons. If you decide to go this route, do not be inhibited by the "expert." Remember that it is your wedding, your reception, your day. You and your groom should have every item exactly as you please, and even though the duties seem as though they never end, don't sacrifice the wedding you want in fear that you and your wedding party could never fulfill all of the responsibilities of it. Good bridal consultants help everything run smoothly; bad ones make everything run their own way.

You've chosen your attendants because of their love

and friendship for you and your groom. Your parents have opted to celebrate with you. As long as the spirit and intentions are positive on everyone's part, all duties will be fulfilled sincerely and willingly.

5

# EXPENSES

*Ethel:* If you'll pay for the champagne and the vintage wine at the reception, I'll dip into my secret savings for the filet mignon.

*Edgar:* If you'll pick up the expense of caviar for the appetizer, I'll take out a loan for the pheasant under glass.

*Both:* (with relief) Somehow, I'm not hungry.

In the last five years a new trend has been seen in the division-of-payments syndrome of wedding expenses. It is a trend that is very positive and encouraging during these troubled economic times. The "Who Pays for What" lists that you will find in magazines and journals may be traditionally correct, but they are not legally binding. More and more weddings today are being paid for jointly by the bride's and groom's families, and many brides and grooms are contributing to their own wedding celebrations. This tendency is easily explained by the number of couples who are both gainfully employed before and after their marriage (close to 90 percent of all brides today plan to work after marrying). It has become more common for both sets of parents to sponsor the wedding, and engagement photographs that are of the couple, rather than just the bride-to-be, exemplify this move in the direction of mutual sharing—right down to paying the bills. The decisions regarding finances are personal ones that you and your families should make together, in private, immediately upon beginning to plan your wedding. If you sit down and discuss all costs openly and honestly, you will be able to work out a budget and divide expenses in a manner acceptable to everyone involved. Have no fear about this type of discussion—it is usually something everyone wants to get clear from the start.

The lists that follow are the conventional division of expenses. Use them as a guide, but remember that you are entitled to split expenses or absorb them all, according to your own situation and your own means. The amount that you spend on any given item is also up to you, and in many instances it is not how much you buy and spend, but how well you shop and purchase that will make your wedding the happy occasion you want it to be. Also, it is the reception rather than the actual wedding that generally becomes the most expensive item. As you budget, keep in mind the fact that a reception can be champagne in the garden or filet mignon in the fanciest hotel in town. The garden may not need to be rented; the hotel will. Decide accordingly. Here is the list of expenses as customarily assigned. The lists, in the manner of this book, are in alphabetical order for your ease and convenience.

The bride or her family pays for:

*1. Church expenses: rental fee, aisle carpet, canopy, tent, sexton's fee.*

*2. Engagement party and photograph.*

*3. Flowers: for the church and reception, bouquets for the honor attendants, bridesmaids, flower girls.*

*4. Gifts for the attendants.*

*5. Groom's wedding ring and wedding gift.*

*6. Hotel accommodations if needed for the bridesmaids, although they may absorb this expense themselves.*

*7. Music: at the reception, the organist's fee at the ceremony, the soloist's fee.*

*8. Photographs.*

*9. Printing: the bride's personal stationery, wedding invitations, announcements, enclosure cards.*

*10. Reception: all costs, food, beverage, room rental.*

*11. Trousseau for the bride.*

*12. Wedding gown, veil, and accessories.*

The groom or his family pays for:

*1. Bride's engagement and wedding rings.*

*2. Clergy fee.*

*3. Flowers: bride's bouquet and going-away corsage, boutonnieres for the men of the wedding party, flowers for the mothers and grandmothers.*

*4. Gifts for the ushers and best man*

*5. Gloves, ties, or ascots, accessories for the men of the wedding party.*

*6. Honeymoon trip.*

*7. Hotel accommodations if needed for the groomsmen, although they may absorb this expense themselves.*

*8. Rehearsal dinner.*

*9. Tuxedo rental for the groom.*

The following are optional expenses; local custom and your own good taste will designate who will pay:

*1. Bachelor's party: usually given by the groomsmen, may be given by the groom himself.*

*2. Bridesmaids' dresses: usually paid for by each attendant herself, may be paid for by the bride.*

*3. Bridesmaids' party: usually given by the bride, may be given by the bridesmaids.*

*4. Flowers: The bride's bouquet may be included in the cost of her ensemble and paid for by her family, although it is traditionally a gift from the groom.*

*The flowers for the bride's mother and grandmother may be purchased by the bride herself rather than the groom. Often the bride and her family pay for all flowers.*

*5. Rehearsal dinner: usually given by the groom's parents, may be given by the bride's friends or relatives.*

*6. Ushers' tuxedo rental charge: usually paid for by each usher himself, may be paid for by the groom.*

This indexing of expenses covers all the charges that you may expect for your wedding celebration. But if you and your groom suddenly discover that you must have something that is, heaven forbid, *not* on the list, do not hesitate to purchase, rent, or hire it. By the same token, if you and your groom decide to eliminate nine tenths of the costs categorized above, go right ahead. What's important is that anything essential to your personal enjoyment on your wedding day be planned for. Keeping within your own budget and getting the most for your money is usually extremely enjoyable.

# 6
# FLOWERS

*Flossie: Oh, Felix, I want the entire church filled with daisies, roses, and chrysanthemums!*

*Felix: Uh, Floss, there's something I forgot to tell you about myself. I don't know why it slipped my mind, it's a condition I've had ever since childhood. I'm . . .*

*Both: (in a tone of sudden realization) Allergic to flowers!*

A good florist is a true artist. This florist is not only experienced in which flowers are suitable for bouquets and centerpieces, but will also share his or her knowledge about which flowers are in season at the time of your wedding and how much your floral needs will cost. A truly creative florist will give you a variety of choices as well as a wide range in price. You may choose a simple bouquet, a single flower for your bridesmaids, and a small boutonniere for the groomsmen, or you may opt to fill the church and reception hall with baskets of flowers and tiers of perennials. Whatever you fancy, make an appointment with your florist at least three months before your wedding day and plan to have him see the reception location before you finalize your order. Be prepared with the information the florist will need to give you an accurate estimate: a description of your dress, the color and style of your attendants' dresses and those of your mothers'; the color and style of your groom's wedding wear, his ushers' and your fathers' (it is very helpful to supply the florist with a sketch of the bridal wear of the party and swatches of fabric for color samples); the color scheme you've chosen for your reception; limitations on what floral arrangements may be placed in the church, or special needs for the church, such as the bouquet traditionally placed at the statue of the Blessed Virgin at Catholic weddings (check with your clergyman). Remember that your florist can usually supply other services, such as the aisle runner, the ring bearer's cushion, canopies, candleholders, and kneeling cushions. Ask which flowers will remain fresh for the longest period of time. If you are watching your budget, make sure to choose flowers that are in season, and ask about the use of greens, which can often be done with great flair and imagination. Request that your florist give you an itemized bill in advance, listing all delivery and setup obligations at both locations —wedding and reception. Make sure that you in turn supply the florist with all names, addresses, and times for delivery. Give him a copy of the maps you make for your guests, even though you have already taken him to the wedding and reception sites. Include directions to your home if you are having photographs taken at home before you leave for the ceremony. You will want your bouquet, your bridesmaid's flowers, and your mother's and father's corsage and boutonniere delivered there if pictures will be taken. Specify exactly which flowers should be delivered where and when. Keep a copy of the list with all of this information for your reference.

If your reception is being held at a hotel or a club, find out if any floral arrangements are included in the overall price. Whether the flowers will be provided by the establishment or if you are having your florist handle the reception, make sure that the centerpieces to be placed on the dining tables are low enough for your guests to see over easily. This is especially true for the bridal table, since your guests will want to be able to see you and your groom during all of the activities of the reception. An arrangement that will be placed at the ceremony or used as decoration away from dining tables will be most effective at eye level or above. The bride and her attendants may arrange their bouquets together to form the centerpiece for the central table or to make a pretty frame for the cake. You may wish to have your bridesmaids and flower girl carry baskets of flowers for this purpose.

Here is a list of the basic floral needs for the ceremony:

*1. The* bride's bouquet *is traditionally white, with a background of greens. The options are numerous, however —you may choose to carry a prayer book with a single flower, a basket of ivy, an arm bouquet of long-stemmed flowers, a crescent-shaped bouquet, or flowers with ribbons and candles for an evening wedding. If you wish to include some color in your bouquet or carry a single long-stemmed red rose, by all means do so.*

*2. Your bridesmaids' flowers may be a nosegay, a basket, a single flower, three small flowers. The important factor is color, and the easiest way to coordinate this element* is to supply an actual swatch of the fabric in which the maid's dresses are made to the florist. It is always a nice touch to have the bridesmaids wear flowers or garlands in their hair instead of headpieces, but consider each hair length and style before making that decision.

*3. The* groom, groomsmen, and both fathers *traditionally wear white carnations, white roses, or white lilies. However, a colorful flower is acceptable and may be used as a coordinating effect with the bridesmaids or with your bouquet.*

*4. Both* mothers and grandmothers *should have corsages that blend with their dresses; they need not be identical.*

*5. You might like to give your musicians and soloist a small floral item to wear during the ceremony. This is a lovely gesture and certainly not mandatory.*

*6. A going-away corsage for yourself is strictly custom, not necessity.*

If you have chosen to have tiny flowers atop your wedding cake, a nice alternative to the bride-and-groom statuette, check to see if your baker or your florist will handle this. It's a very attractive touch to have a small blossom or little buds attached with ribbons to the cake-cutting knife.

Usually, the flowers that decorate the church remain there and are donated for the next Sunday's services. Seldom are the flowers carried to the reception, although there is no strict ruling. If you plan to have a large amount of flowers at the reception, it is very generous of you to designate someone to transport them to hospitals, old-age homes, or other charities after the festivities. That way, the beauty and tranquility that the flowers brought to your wedding day may be shared with many others after you and your friends have enjoyed them.

7

# GUEST LISTS

*Greta: My mother wanted one hundred guests and said if his mother didn't like inviting her fifty, she could, as the old expression goes, lump it.*

*George: My mother wanted one hundred guests of her own and said there had to be a way to go to my wedding without speaking to my future mother-in-law.*

*Both: We eloped.*

Here's an ideal situation: You plan your wedding, you are able to invite an unlimited number of guests, you divide that number by two, and it is exactly the number that your family and your groom's family each want to invite to the festivities!

Here's another ideal situation: As you plan your wedding, you make a list of every person you could possibly want to come to your wedding. Your groom and his family make the same kind of list. You check the lists against one another, find that the duplications are minimal, and that when you tally the total, the lists are exactly equal in number. You add those two numbers together, include the number of duplicates, come up with the grand total, and find that it is just what your budget can handle.

Here's a third ideal situation: You and your groom and your families agree that you would like to have a small wedding. You and your groom each make a list of guests that you would like to invite and have no trouble on deciding upon twenty names each. Every relative and friend that you both ever wanted at the wedding is included.

Now, let's get back to reality. Your guest list will be the determining factor for all of the logistics of your wedding, from the choice of site for the ceremony to the number of meals served at the reception. You can start with estimating the greatest number of persons you will be able to invite to your wedding and then cut back if necessary. By setting an outside limit, you will be able to control the great temptation of adding just one friend here and just one distant relative there. As you compile your lists, take into account those friends who live too far away to be able to attend, but remember that if an invitation (rather than an announcement) is sent, you must be prepared to welcome that guest to all eating, drinking, dancing, and merriment that will take place. There are four important elements in the making of guest lists: deciding how many guests you can afford to invite, choosing who you want to invite, determining who you must invite (hopefully, these three factors will become one and the same), and finding the best method for keeping records regarding those you have invited.

The best device for keeping all of your records regarding guests in order is a simple file box with three- by five-inch cards, dividers, and an alphabetical index. Each guest who will be sent an invitation should be given his or her own card. Use one card for a family or for couples that will be invited. Include on the card the name of each person invited, including all children, and make a note of the number of persons in the top right-hand corner. You will be able to total easily. Include the full address with Zip code, and the telephone number if available. Decide on a notation system that will clearly distinguish if the guest is to receive an invitation to the wedding, an invitation to the wedding and reception, or an announcement. You may wish to divide the cards into these three categories and alphabetize each group separately. Designate a space for date sent and for acceptance or regret if the person is invited to the reception. You may choose to write "yes" or "no" next to the number that you've placed in the right-hand corner; if a few, but not all, members of a family will attend, you might note this number in a different color ink beside the number invited. Because each invited guest will have a card, you will be able to sort them easily into acceptances and regrets for quick totaling.

These cards may also be used to record information on gifts that are sent; you can record the date you receive the gift, a brief description of the item, and the date you send your thank-you card. Some people use a notebook for recording information on guests, especially if the wedding will be small—fifty persons or fewer. The cards are a bit more convenient to handle because you can sort them and change their order as frequently as necessary. Decide on a method that will work best for you, but do not mail any invitations without some form of record. If you establish your system and use it from the very beginning of your wedding planning, you will provide yourself with one of the most valuable tools for organization of the event.

Traditionally, the bride and groom share the guest list in equal number. However, the sponsors of the wedding are the ones who decide the actual number of guests that may be invited. If the bride's parents are sponsoring the wedding, they should ask the groom's family to provide them with a list of names, with full addresses, of the guests they wish to invite; the invitations will be addressed and sent by the bride's family. They should be given a specific number of guests that they will be able to invite, and a specific date by which the bride's family will need the complete list. If this is the situation in which you find yourself, remember to ask your groom's family for a list of persons to whom they wish an announcement sent, if you have decided to send announcements. No matter who sponsors the wedding, it is best to have a brief meeting to discuss all of these details; all of the parties involved should be aware of the number of guests that will be invited. One family may have to cut back, but before this is done, the other family may not need as many invitational places, so those spots may be used by the family that does need them. The only way to handle this matter quickly and diplomatically is for each family to express their feelings, exercising understanding in the case of a family who wishes to sponsor the wedding but has limited means to do so. In the case of divorced parents, it is customary that the parent who raised the child retain the invitation privilege. However, make sure that all of the relatives and friends who have remained close to you (or your groom, if this is his situation) are not overlooked.

There are a few people who should be on your guest list right from the start, and it is best to begin your list with them and then decide on the number of places that will remain. Your officiator and his or her spouse are invited to the reception. The husbands and wives of your married attendants are invited. If any of your attendants are engaged, their mate-to-be is invited. The parents of your flower girl and ring bearer are invited. All the members of your immediate family and of your groom's immediate family, as well as all of your attendants, should be sent an invitation to the wedding and reception, even though they were probably the first people involved in the planning of the affair. After you've listed all of these people and tallied your count thus far, you can begin to add your other guests. Once you've taken care of the "musts" there will probably be plenty of "maybes" to decide upon. You may wish to invite the parents of your attendants. You will have to think about neighbors who have become friends due only to proximity. There may be business associates or even loyal local merchants whom you feel compelled to consider. If your guest list will be small, it is sometimes wise to eliminate an entire group rather than try to decide which members should or should not be invited. A good example of this is the group of people that you and your groom each work with. It is better not to invite anyone rather than offend some or embarrass others. Tact and diplomacy will serve as your guides; think of each and every guest individually as you add or subtract their name from your list. If you start to hear the expression "If we invite her, we've got to invite him" more often than you would like, it might be time to cut back.

This is also the moment to decide if the printing of wedding announcements will be of value to you. They serve as a wonderful gesture of sharing the good news, informing people who would either want or need to know of your marriage. The sending of an announcement often replaces the obligation of actually extending an invitation to a person who you really are not able to invite, or whom you would not expect to attend the wedding.

There are two situations which are often confusing in regard to guest lists. First, if you plan to invite a guest to bring a guest to your wedding, ask your friend for the name and address of the person and send an invitation to that person. Not only is this proper and courteous, but it will provide you with an address to which you can send a thank-you note, since that person will probably bring a gift. The second situation that is often misunderstood is in regard to gifts. A wedding invitation requires a response only if an invitation to a reception is included. A wedding announcement does not require an acknowledgment. Neither a wedding invitation nor an announcement requires a gift. Only if the guest intends to be present at the festivities should a gift be expected, and technically speaking, even then it is not an obligation. You are doing the inviting, or the announcing, to ask friends to join you at a celebration or to inform them of the news. You are not asking for a gift. Unfortunately, guests often misunderstand your intentions, and you may have friends whose presence at your wedding is far more important to you than the giving of a gift. There may be other persons who feel obliged to spend an amount that is beyond their means, when you and your groom would be perfectly content with a small memento. By the same token, you will probably receive gifts from people who are unable to attend the wedding and sometimes from persons who were not even invited. Being gracious and sincere and prompt in your expression of thanks is the correct thing to do in all of these circumstances.

Remember that guest lists are not sacred and are not bound by time. If you suddenly remember someone whose name you truly forgot, do not hesitate to add that person to your list. However, once an invitation is extended, it cannot be rescinded, so be sure that you feel positive about everyone on your list. Just ask yourselves one question: "Do we want this person to be present at one of the most important events of our lives?" You and your groom will know the answer and will proceed to compile your guest list with great ease.

# 8
# HONEYMOONS

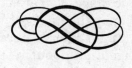

*Harriet: It's monsoon season in the tropics at that time of year!*

*Horace: Well, sweetie, you're the one who said Quebec is not quaint when it's under six feet of snow.*

*Both: (Gleefully) No one will ever know we're home if we unplug the phone and don't answer the door for a week.*

Where your reception demands that you be concerned with the enjoyment and comfort of your guests, your honeymoon is the time that you need be concerned only with the enjoyment and comfort of you and your husband.

Regardless of any enticing photographs depicting exotic islands that you may see in magazines or pamphlets, do not feel obliged to travel great distances to a place whose name you cannot even pronounce. The most important factor is your own "luxury," even if this means three days of elegance in your own downtown hotel with no plane ride at all!

As with all of your other wedding plans, make your honeymoon reservations well in advance. A good travel agent can be invaluable, and many experienced agents have journeyed to the places you are considering. Another point of reference may be friends who have recently visited resorts you might like. It is extremely helpful to have firsthand information about restaurants and entertainment your friends have enjoyed. The whole world is at your doorstep; what may not be at your doorstep are hotel rooms in a honeymoon spot that you set your heart upon. And it could be that your doorstep will be extremely costly. Let timing be your guide. Check off-season prices, super-saver air fares (which *must* be reserved and purchased in advance), special excursion rates, night-flight discounts. Your travel agent can inform you about all the special honeymoon packages that are available all year round. Even if you and your husband are experienced travelers (perhaps you both travel often for business), it is wise to engage the services of a good travel agent who will make all of your reservations and arrangements and provide you with a written itinerary for your entire journey. These papers are a must, and you should include them with the other important valuables you will take with you—passports, travelers' checks, medication, hotel and flight confirmation slips—and keep in your hand tote or purse in case luggage is lost or delayed.

As you make your plans and choices, remember the basics—meals, housing, and transportation to, from, and during your holiday. A complete honeymoon package usually takes care of all of these details, and often a hotel or country inn will include one or more meals per day. A "bed and breakfast" accommodation is a charming way to save money on sustenance, thereby allowing for more of a splurge in a restaurant for your evening meal. Often breakfast will be quite substantial (the innkeeper's reputation for cuisine relies upon it) and will save you time and tide you through the day until dinner. However, remember that there can always be too much of a good thing, and in many resort hotels the complete plan of three full meals is mandatory, can be quite expensive, and is usually more food than any human being can consume in one day. This type of service is called the Full American Plan. The Modified American Plan, which includes breakfast and limited dinner menu, provides a third alternative. The fourth choice regarding meals is the European Plan. This means going it completely on your own, choosing and locating restaurants or shopping for food and drink at local groceries and markets. Unless your room is equipped with cooking facilities, and assuming that you wish to use vacation time for food preparation, it is difficult to count on eating anything more than cold snacks in your room.

Reconfirm your hotel reservations two weeks before arrival, checking everything from bathroom accommodations to type and size of beds. Don't be shy about revealing your newlywed status; most hotels will extend extra courtesies to you, and your reservation will most likely be handled with and designated for special consideration. If any problems arise, waste no time—ask to speak directly to the manager or the first assistant manager. Most hotels have a policy to deal with rooms that are not ready at the appointed hour of reservation. They will usually make arrangements for equivalent accommodations elsewhere for the time it takes to correct the situation, and should provide round-trip taxi fare from their establishment to the alternate location.

If you will be departing from any town or city on your itinerary after hotel checkout time, you can usually check your luggage with the bell captain in the reception area or request in advance that checkout time be extended. Always allow extra time to check out of any hotel, especially when you will be making a plane or train departure at a specific hour.

It is helpful to make a list of everything you wish to pack for your honeymoon, especially if you will be going to a place with climate and temperature very different from your own. You don't want to forget your bathing suit or your ski parka. You might designate a special place where you can assemble everything you need; keep in mind the advantage of limiting yourself to two bags per person. If you do so, you can take one bag on board for travel and check the other, and probably manage to carry both by yourself if necessary. Do leave a bit of empty room in your larger suitcase for souvenirs that you will purchase on your trip. Check that you have a claim check for every piece of luggage that leaves your hands, and if your baggage is lost or damaged, do not leave the airport without reporting the loss and completing the necessary forms.

If you prepare for any possible emergencies, chances are you probably won't have any. Start by making sure that you have an adequate supply of any medications you may need, especially if you or your mate are prone to any allergies. If you do become ill during your trip, contact the house physician of the hotel where you are staying or obtain the number for the office of the International Association for Medical Assistance nearest you. If you lose your passport or visa, immediately contact the U.S. consulate and make a report. Keep a record of your passport number and travelers' checks in a place other than your wallet in case of loss or theft. If you find you are running short of funds, call or cable for an international draft to be sent; be aware of any advantages that your various credit cards may provide in this situation. Some card holders are entitled to draw against their account without a check or other previous arrangements. If you arrive at your sunny destination and it rains for seven days straight, inquire about movies, indoor activities, and sightseeing from buses. Rain or shine, do not panic if you both do not want to participate in the exact same activity at every waking moment. If he's dying to go fishing and loathes boutiques, and you can't bear the smell of bait and must bring your cousin Suzy a gift, just arrange to take the time that each of you needs for some private moments. You'll enjoy your time together all the more. Avoid any travel confusion by reconfirming your flights twenty-four hours in advance for domestic travel and seventy-two hours in advance for transoceanic destinations.

An action-packed honeymoon may be exactly what you do not need. You've just been through some very hectic months planning and celebrating your wedding reception, so don't overexert yourselves on these first few days alone together. Don't allow fatigue, which is absolutely natural and should be expected, to alarm you if either or both of you don't feel up to lots of activity, intimate or public. The heart-shaped bathtub can wait until you both feel energetic enough to enjoy it. In fact, you may decide not to leave for your honeymoon trip on the day of your wedding. A decision to delay your departure is strictly up to you. On the other hand, if your only escape to solitude is a honeymoon haven miles and miles away, you may leave directly from your reception and get there as quickly as possible. Your exit from your reception signals the beginning of the end of the festivities, and it should also signify the beginning of a joyous and private time for you and your new spouse.

# 9

# I DO!—
# THE CEREMONY

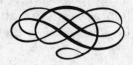

*Irma: I, I, I . . . get . . . so, so, nervous at the thought of speaking before a large crowd of people . . . !*

*Ivan: I don't. I thought I'd read a few poems, then sing a song after the rings, do a couple of readings before the recessional. Irma, what's the matter, honey? You're crying. Oh . . . OK . . . how about this. We'll just say two words, alright? Now, show me that big smile and give this a try. . . .*

*Both: I do!*

You may attend many parties over the years, and your own wedding reception will probably be one of the best. But your wedding ceremony is an official act, a singularly important event that only happens once in your life. It is a rite that includes the exchange of vows which will be recognized legally and which will signify permanence. And it is the surrounding of this happy, yet serious, ceremony with too many "hearts and flowers" that can disguise its true meaning. For no matter how elaborate or simple your celebration may be, the one common denominator in all weddings is the exchange of marriage vows in an official, ceremonial setting. A wedding ceremony can be a long, traditional, formal function or a short recitation of promises, but no matter what you choose, the music, readings, speeches, and sermons should reemphasize, not camouflage, the exchange of wedding vows. This can be accomplished with beauty and taste and will be a moment (for it only takes a few minutes for two people to take an oath) that you and your groom will never forget, one that your friends and relatives will be thrilled to witness. It can also be totally enjoyable.

First, decide with your officiator which parts of the marriage ceremony are obligatory. Every religion has its own official procedures, as does the typical civil ceremony. Once you've determined what's essential, you will have the basis to formulate a ceremony that will reflect your own personal feelings and beliefs. You may choose to have the traditional ceremony performed word for word, for it may express exactly what you and your groom feel about the solemnity of the occasion. Review the traditional ceremony in its entirety to make sure this is what you wish for public proclamation of your commitment. You may choose to do a bit of rewriting to make the ceremony more personal to you and your spouse; get your clergy member's approval, but do not hesitate to make these changes. If you will choose prose and poems, or if friends will compose speeches, have these readings given in full at the rehearsal or before, in case you wish to modify them.

Every word should support your point of view. As simplistic as this may appear, some of the newer ceremonies have been known to confuse the issue. Just make sure that all your guests, including older relatives, do comprehend that the vows have been officially taken, no matter how intricate or elaborate the text of your ceremony becomes. Also, make sure that all your guests can see the entire ceremony.

You may wish to have your guests participate actively in your ceremony. Perhaps they can form a circle around you, your groom, and your officiator as you take your vows. You may wish to designate a moment in the ceremony when you and your groom extend the traditional sign of peace, a kiss or a handshake, that you will give to your attendants and to the person on the end of each aisle to pass down the line of guests in that row. Remember that people who are of a different religious affiliation may not understand, or may not feel able, to join in a recitation or kneel at a certain moment. An announcement from your officiator can clear up any misunderstanding; some couples even have souvenir programs printed that include the entire ceremony as well as any directions for the congregation. As for a religious belief that would prohibit participation in good conscience by a guest, simply provide a comfortable place for this guest to remain silent and witness the ceremony more passively than your other guests. If you and your groom each have a strong religious affiliation, but are of different faiths, you might consider asking your respective clergy members to both participate in a service of an ecumenical nature. You may wish to have both of your parents and your groom walk in the processional, a traditional Jewish custom. The trend has been toward a more active participation in wedding ceremonies by all persons present, symbolizing the sharing of love and friendship.

The planning of your ceremony will take time and

thought, so make sure you schedule for it. Once you have made your decisions, type a copy of the full ceremony, go to your officiator for agreement on it, and make copies for everyone from honor attendants to musicians to use at rehearsal. If you will recite rather than repeat your vows, they will be even more meaningful if you memorize them.

There are three elements involved in the planning of your ceremony—the ceremony itself, from beginning to end; the rehearsal of it (which is a must); and the transportation to it. If one were to make an outline of the traditional ceremony, it would read like this: the arriving and seating of guests, seating of family, processional, the giving away of the bride or some other family gesture, words of welcome and prayer or meditation, exchange of vows, giving of rings, pronouncement of marriage, words or action (a kiss or blessing) of closing, and recessional.

If you will be married in a church with a center aisle, everyone will go to their seats via this route, unless you choose to put an aisle carpet in place before the arrival of any of your guests. In this case, your guests are escorted to their places by the side aisles. You may choose to have the aisle carpet rolled into place after the mother of the bride is seated; she is the last person to enter the church and her presence signals that the ceremony is about to begin. If your church has more than one major aisle, choose the one that is most convenient; if there are two aisles, you may wish to use one for the processional and one for the recessional. If you are using an aisle carpet at all, and choose to decorate only one aisle, it should be the processional aisle.

At least forty-five minutes to an hour before the scheduled time of the ceremony, the ushers should be at the church in complete wedding attire. Any music should start a half hour before the ceremony; customarily, a soloist or choir does not usually sing until just before the processional music. However, the bride may wish to have a special song sung as her mother is seated, or the couples may wish to have songs sung during the seating of guests. The bridesmaids, fully dressed right to their flowers, should be at the church fifteen to thirty minutes prior to the ceremony, and they should have a private place to wait. The groom and his best man should arrive at this time as well; they usually wait in the vestry of the church or some other small anteroom from which they will enter the church directly for the service. The bride and her father are the last to arrive, but should be present ten to fifteen minutes before the beginning of the ceremony. Some wedding parties use rooms at the church for dressing; obviously, this eliminates the need to schedule arrivals close to the time of the ceremony, but may prove limiting in space for making up, storing street clothing, and having access to bathroom facilities.

The ushers will seat every guest; they greet the guests and ask if they are friends of the bride or of the groom. The bride's guests sit on the left side of the church and the groom's sit on the right. If either the bride or groom have a much larger number of guests than the other, the ushers should be instructed to seat guests equally on both sides. At smaller weddings, guests may seat themselves. If there will be reserved seating, the head usher should be given a list of these guests or shown a copy of the pew card if they have been sent. If pew ribbons are used to designate reserved sections, they should be removed by the ushers as the pews fill. The usher offers his right arm to the feminine guests, and husbands or male escorts follow. If a group of women enter together, each should be escorted by an usher, and the usher who escorts the oldest woman should lead the way. Approximately five minutes before the ceremony begins, brothers and sisters of the bride and groom are escorted to the pews directly behind their parents. Next, the groom's parents are seated in the first pew on the right; the father of the groom takes the aisle seat. Finally, the mother of the bride is seated in the first pew on the left, leaving the aisle seat for the father of the bride. Just before escorting the mother of the bride to her place, the head usher goes to the vestry to alert the groom and his best man that the ceremony will begin momentarily. The bride's mother may be escorted by her own son, rather than the head usher, if the brother of the bride is a member of the wedding party. She is the last person to be seated before the ceremony begins. Aisle ribbons if desired, are put in place at this point, and the aisle carpet is rolled out by two ushers. The groom, his best man, and the officiator take their places.

The processional is about to begin; this can be signified with the introduction of the processional music. In most churches, guests stand for the procession, and the mother of the bride can give the cue for this; guests will follow suit. The bridesmaids enter first, walking singly. They are followed by the ushers, also walking one by one.

For the most part, the old hesitation step has been abandoned for a more natural, slow walking style. If there are children in the wedding party, they enter next—the ring bearer followed by the flower girl, who traditionally precedes the bride and showers flower petals upon her path. The bride waits to enter until all of her attendants are at least halfway down the aisle, or she may wait until they have reached the altar. The bride must decide whether to take her father's left or right arm; if she takes his right, he will not have to cross behind her to return to his pew on the left side of the church, and this will facilitate matters. However, the bride may ask both of her parents to escort her down the aisle, one on each side. Or the bride and groom may decide to walk down the aisle hand in hand. If the bride's father is deceased, she may ask an uncle, her brother, a close relative, or her mother to accompany her down the aisle. It is helpful to have a friend at the back of the church to straighten and fluff the train of the bride's wedding gown just before she walks down the aisle. When the bride reaches the altar, she hands her bouquet to her maid of honor. The ceremony begins. The officiator will speak the words of welcome and may give signals throughout the ceremony for the guests to sit or stand. If the bride wishes to be given away, when the officator asks "Who gives this woman in marriage?" her father may answer, "Her mother and I." Or her parents may respond together, "We do." Or the bride may choose to eliminate the tradition of giving away entirely The "main event" of the exchange of vows will take place, and is proceeded or followed by whatever readings or sermons have been chosen. Songs may also be interspersed at appropriate moments, the number and selections having been planned in advance. When it is time to give each other rings, the bride and groom take the rings from their respective honor attendants and either hand them to the officiator for a blessing or give the rings directly to each other, speaking whatever words or statements have been selected for this moment. The officiator will conclude the ceremony with the pronouncement of marriage and whatever closing has been chosen. The recessional follows and is essentially the processional in reverse. The maid of honor gives the bride her bouquet and adjusts her train; the bride takes her groom's right arm and they exit first. The flower girl and ring bearer follow, then the maid of honor takes the best man's right arm and they exit. The bridesmaids and ushers then follow in pairs, a symbol of the marital union that has just been made, the ladies on the right arms of the men. If there are more ushers than bridesmaids, or vice versa, the ladies may exit in pairs and are followed by the men in pairs. If there is an odd number of attendants, one will have to brave the exit alone. Ushers may return to escort mothers, grandmothers, and older feminine relatives of the bride and groom, but usually the bride's parents exit together, immediately after the wedding party, and are followed by the groom's parents. Guests will do the same, alternating left and right, row by row, to exit. If no reception is scheduled, the receiving line may form in the vestibule of the church (with the clergy member's permission), and the guests may immediately offer their best wishes.

Everything that has just been described, with the exception of your guests, really must be rehearsed. The only way to guarantee order, smoothness, and timing is to rehearse the ceremony. Everyone—the bride, groom, officiator, musicians, soloists, attendants, and participating parents—should attend the rehearsal. The rehearsal is usually directed by the officiator, but do not be embarrassed to speak up if anything is unclear or if you or your groom wish to make changes. At the rehearsal, all signals and cues for the running of the ceremony should be set, the order and spacing of the processional and recessional should be decided, and the groupings and movements for and during the ceremony should be planned. It is extremely helpful for the participants to hear the processional and recessional music so the pace of their step can be determined. If a ceremony will vary greatly from tradition, rehearsal is even more essential. The ushers should be briefed on their duties and informed of any unusual arrangements in seating. The entire wedding party should become familiar with the interior of the church, including the location of entrances, exits, the vestry, and waiting rooms. A wedding rehearsal can be very pleasant—the people involved are certainly those closest to the bride and groom, and the rehearsal will provide that sense of relief in knowing that everyone is well informed of their duties and feels confident in performing them. The wedding rehearsal should be scheduled for the evening before or two nights before the wedding, no further in advance than that. This will insure that all the details are fresh in everyone's mind and will make scheduling a bit easier for those people arriving from out of town.

Transportation on the day of days may mean traveling only a few miles, but scheduling is imperative. You may decide to hire drivers and limousines (if so, make reservations well in advance) or you may choose to enlist the aid of friends and relatives with cars. If you choose the latter, offer to pay for gas and give a small thank-you gift if the person makes special trips or goes beyond the call of duty. For a large wedding, four limousines are usually hired. Three cars go to the bride's home, if the bridesmaids will dress there (this is often arranged so photographs may be taken there before leaving for the ceremony). The first transports the bride and her father, the second the mother of the bride and a close relative or friend (possibly the maid of honor), and the third car is for the bridesmaids. The fourth car transports the groom and his best man from wherever they are dressing. These cars wait at the church and at the end of the ceremony, the bride and groom are driven to the reception in the first car, the parents of the bride in the second, the best man and maid of honor in the third, and the bridesmaids in the fourth. This plan is certainly flexible; you may decide to have only one chauffeur-driven car for you and your father to go to the wedding and you, your groom, and your parents to go to the reception. You might plan to have your ushers arrange transportation for the bridesmaids from the church to the reception. Whether you use the services of a limousine company or that of friends, make sure all the drivers have written instructions for where they are to be, whom they are to transport, and when they must be at each location. Include specific addresses of the church, reception, and homes where people will be picked up, and supply any maps that may be necessary.

Don't forget to make arrangements for transportation after the reception, especially for people who will ride in limousines to the church and reception. If you plan to use your groom's car for the honeymoon getaway, make sure that it gets to the reception; the best man could be responsible for this. If you will have a large number of out-of-town guests, it is wise to assign friends to pick them up or to lead the way if the guests have their own automobiles. Those friends can be available to the out-of-town guests throughout the day to give directions or offer any needed assistance. You may need to contact your local police and arrange for traffic control and parking attendants if your wedding will be very large. Make arrangements in advance for additional parking space if your wedding will be held at home.

Your wedding ceremony is the essence of your marriage, the reason for all other activities you will schedule. The words "plan in advance" strictly apply to your ceremony as well as your reception, and this includes everyone's getting to the church on time and knowing exactly what to do once they get there. Whether extremely traditional or completely unique, the ceremony at which you and your groom say "I do" should be an event you've anticipated with great excitement, because you've planned and rehearsed with great care.

# 10
# JEWELS
# AND JEWELERS

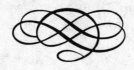

*Jacqueline: It's exquisite, honey, but do you really think I'd get much use out of this diamond tiara?*

*Jasper: I absolutely love it, darling, but I don't know if this ruby pendant will look right with my everyday business suit.*

*Both: (As the jeweler approaches) How about basic gold rings?*

Jewelry is as personal as your own wardrobe and, in the case of engagement and wedding rings, as cherished as your most valuable treasures, regardless of monetary value. However, any jewelry purchase is a true investment and one that should involve three people only—you, your husband-to-be, and the most reputable jeweler you can find. Your engagement and wedding rings are gifts from your groom to you; his wedding ring is a gift from you to him. But discuss your feelings about the subject before getting out your checkbook. Perhaps neither of you really wants an engagement ring, and there is no reason to invest time and money in the search if this is the case. Perhaps you would like an engagement ring, but have never been overly fond of diamonds. Or maybe you would prefer a beautiful bracelet or another piece of jewelry entirely rather than the traditional engagement present of a diamond ring. Whatever you decide, it is wise to choose the items together unless you are absolutely certain of exactly what type and style of jewelry your mate would desire. You are the ones who will wear the rings, probably on a daily basis, so they should be items that you would choose for yourselves to enjoy from the first moment of wear on. As much fun as a surprise gift can be, there is nothing worse than being forced to wear something you truly do not care for, or to have a gift of jewelry sit in its box in a drawer for posterity.

The world of jewelry includes many beautiful gems for your engagement keepsake; you are certainly not limited to diamonds. Any of the birthstones make lovely mementos, and solid gold and sterling silver can be worn in a variety of ways. If a diamond is your choice, your jeweler will discuss the four *C*'s—carat weight, clarity, color, and cut. In today's market prices vary constantly, but the financial benefits for the future must be considered. Large diamonds are becoming more rare, so many jewelers will recommend that for investment purposes you do not shy away from all sizes of diamonds when you begin shopping. Remember that every diamond is different and that many people are fooled by ring settings. Keep the two distinct in your mind, because the setting for a stone is a totally separate issue from the value of the stone itself. There was a guide recommended by financial analysts that used to advise you to spend no more than three weeks salary, or 6 percent of your annual income, on a diamond ring. However, our economy has changed dramatically, and the price of a half-carat diamond can go as high as three thousand dollars. This investment could prove to be one of the wisest you'll make during your married life, so you may choose to spend some savings and "shop big." On the other hand, a small point diamond can make a very pretty, simple engagement ring. Request that all details concerning the gem you purchase be put in writing and included with your receipt by your jeweler —the exact weight if it is a diamond, the quality of the stone, whether any synthetic materials are included. The Federal Trade Commission has established regulations that apply specifically to the jewelry industry. Any honest and forthright jeweler will permit you to take a piece to an appraiser of your choice for confirmation of value. Before you finalize your purchase, make sure that you are aware of all return policies and all guarantees. Have these put in writing as well, and immediately insure all of your purchases. When storing your diamond, remember to keep it separate from other items in your jewelry case. Diamonds are the hardest substance known to man, and they could easily scratch your other softer metals and stones.

Heirloom rings have always been a popular and beautiful gesture of giving. If you or your fiancé have an heirloom jewel in your family, it is perfectly acceptable to wear it as your engagement or wedding ring. The ring should be resized and may need resetting; your fiancé pays for this.

Your wedding ring is worn on the third finger of your left hand. If you do choose to wear an engagement ring, it is worn on the left hand until you are married; you may then wear it on your right hand after the wedding (remember to wear it on the right hand for the actual ceremony). You may select an engagement ring that interlocks with a wedding band. If you opt for this, make sure your groom has both rings before the ceremony. Keep this possibility in mind when selecting your rings, and remember, too, that you will probably wish to wear your engagement ring along with your wedding band long after your wedding, not just during the engagement period. Choose each ring to complement the other. Your wedding band and that of your groom may match, although this is not mandatory. It is far more important that the rings be meaningful and comfortable, something each of you has chosen. Wedding bands are usually engraved; not only is this a special personal touch for the gifts you are giving each other, but in a very practical sense, the engraving serves as identification in case of loss or theft.

During the actual wedding ceremony, watches are not worn by any wedding party members. Tradition affirms that on this day, time does not matter. Your bridesmaids may wear very simple earrings and discreet jewelry, if any. Your gift to your attendants may be a specific item of jewelry that they will wear for the wedding ceremony. Brides do not wear heavy bracelets or necklaces; your gown and headpiece will provide a total look that will not require numerous accessories.

Your jewel and jewelry options are many. Take all the time you need to shop for these items; it may turn into precious hours for you and your groom to be alone as things get hectic before the big day. Remember that there are private artisans in every city, so if you have a very specific design in mind, you may wish to have your rings made by a local goldsmith or silversmith who specializes in exclusive designs. This alternative to the very large display cases filled with hundreds of engagement and wedding bands can usually be located through the nearest art museum or local gallery. Do check recommendations, ask to see samples, and get every detail in writing before deposit or purchase.

More and more grooms are wearing rings today, a tradition that had previously been upheld only by brides. The first decision in this mutual giving is whether to wear rings at all, a choice that is strictly up to the two of you. Once you've decided, your wedding rings will serve as symbols of your mutual sharing for years after your wedding, whether they be solid gold bands or charms from a bubble-gum machine. It is truly the thought (and wise purchasing) that counts.

## 11
# KINDS OF WEDDINGS

*Kitty: There is only one kind of wedding to have.*

*Kermit: I totally agree, my dear.*

*Both: Ours.*

When you and your groom begin to consider what kind of wedding you want to have, there are a myriad of types and styles to choose from, or you can invent your very own. There used to be all sorts of rules and regulations about when, what, and where a wedding should be, but now the choices are yours and the possibilities are almost limitless. You can opt to have a traditional kind of wedding, you can select certain elements from one kind of wedding and combine them with facets of another, or you can be the originator of a brand-new kind of wedding. There are really only two factors to keep in mind at all times: that you make sure all legal aspects of the exchange of marriage vows are handled, and that you and your guests are comfortable and happy because of the taste and discernment you'll use in planning the event.

If you answer the following questions, you will come up with the kind of wedding you want: where you want to be married, when—the date and hour, how much you wish to spend, what type of reception you want, how many guests you wish to invite, and whether the locations involved and personnel needed will be available on the date you choose. It sounds simple, this short listing of items, but once you've dealt with each of them, you will have your entire wedding planned!

The traditional kinds of weddings described below exemplify the basic categories available to you. Feel free to pick and choose, mix and match, until you come up with exactly the kind of wedding you and your groom desire. The degree of formality is entirely up to you—you may wish to have a very small, quiet ceremony and a large, lavish reception.

If you decide to be married on a rocky hillside, you may not be able to set up a buffet table and will need to choose a different location for the reception. You may want to follow a traditional ceremony with a picnic dinner.

Combine common sense with good taste, and remember, no matter who pays the bills, it is vital that you and your groom have the kind of wedding that you will both enjoy.

## The Formal Wedding

A formal wedding is usually very large; the guest list numbers anywhere from fifty to five hundred, and averages at approximately two hundred. (The tendency is to have more than two hundred guests rather than less.) There should be an usher for each fifty guests, so the bridal party itself is large. A formal wedding is held at a church, synagogue, or hotel, with all the accoutrements: limousines, formal portraits (both engagement and wedding), as well as continuous candid picture taking, lots of flowers, engraved invitations, announcements, at-home cards, reception cards, opulent wedding gown and bridal wear, and a traditional, often lengthy, ceremony. The reception is also quite large; a full meal is served, musicians are hired, drink often flows freely, and the customary activities of first dance, toasting, and cake cutting are overseen by a master of ceremonies.

## The Semiformal Wedding

A semiformal wedding is usually smaller than a formal one, and the primary difference between the two is the degree of fanciness or lavishness. At a semiformal wedding a long or short dress, or even a dressy suit, may be worn, the ceremony may not be quite as traditional as a formal one, and full portraits may be eliminated from the picture taking. The trimmings of the ceremony—pew ribbons, aisle carpets, canopies—are often omitted when a long dress and train are not worn. Since the wedding party itself is smaller, a flower girl and ring bearer are often not included. The reception may be only champagne and hors d'oeuvres rather than a full sit-down meal, and the music may be recorded rather than live. The reception may even be held at the bride's or groom's home.

## The Informal Wedding

An informal wedding usually includes only fifty to seventy-five invitees and may even be much smaller than that in number of guests. It is the most flexible type of wedding because it may be held anywhere; a gathering of such a small group permits this. Invitations are often handwritten; the bride may wear flowers in her hair, but not carry a full bouquet; guests usually seat themselves; and the bride and groom often mingle with them before and immediately after the short ceremony. Processionals, recessionals, and traditional trimmings are not included in the ceremony. The small reception may be held at home, and the families might decide to prepare all of the food themselves.

Remember that these three kinds of weddings are categories of varying levels of formality. You may decide to have an informal wedding for 250 people, or you might plan a formal wedding for 40 guests. These decisions are completely up to you. The following examples will demonstrate just a few of the choices that might be planned by you and your families; each may be as formal or informal as you desire.

### Garden Weddings

Garden weddings may be planned for any level of formality, but keep your practical side in mind. If you need to walk down a rocky garden path, you won't want a long train. Garden weddings usually do include some form of processional, but a recessional is eliminated—the bride and groom turn to their guests immediately following the ceremony or are joined by parents and attendants to form a receiving line on the site of the wedding. You might use a tent or canopy, and if the weather becomes extremely inclement, you might wish to move all of the festivities inside. Inside should be nearby.

## At-Home Weddings

At-home weddings are usually informal because they are small, but if "at home" for you is a twenty-room estate, you might be planning formal festivities and certainly may do so. If you do wish to have your wedding at home, and need to expand on space, consider a tent or canopy. Many people who plan at-home weddings do so for budgetary reasons or because they wish to do all of the cooking and preparation themselves; you could also hire a caterer to do so. At-home weddings often include buffets rather than sit-down dinners, which are usually difficult in the average home for groups larger than thirty persons. You could still designate a bridal table, a parent's table, a special table for the wedding cake, and a separate bar area. If you decide to do the cooking, plan a trial run before the big day. Test each item in advance, check the time you will need for preparation, and by all means taste everything.

## Civil Ceremonies

A civil ceremony is usually categorized as informal and is celebrated in the same fashion as an informal wedding. However, a civil ceremony may be followed by a very large, formal reception (the same day or later). Often, due strictly to preference, a couple may choose to be married by a civil officiator under otherwise formal circumstances.

The *when* of your wedding will affect the *where* far more greatly than any other detail. Even though strict regulation, for the most part, has been cast aside, check with your officiator or clergy member for any limitations.

Jewish weddings are not held on Saturdays (the Sabbath) and certain holy days. Christian weddings do not usually take place on Christmas or Easter; Catholic weddings are often not scheduled during Lent. In Catholic churches, most weddings take place on Saturday, and the full nuptial mass is not celebrated between the hours of three and six P.M. because this is the time reserved for the hearing of confessions in the parish. Local parish rulings should be investigated before choosing the hour for your wedding. Aside from these standard rules, which are followed at all times, the other practical factor to consider is the reservation of a specific hour for weddings other than your own. This is especially prevalent during the more popular weddings months of June, August, September, and December. Therefore, as soon as you make the choice of where and when you wish to hold your wedding ceremony and celebrate your wedding reception, contact the persons responsible for scheduling these locations.

Let your imagination run wild or your love of tradition prevail as you plan the kind of wedding you wish to have. Even if you have to have the miniversion because of a limited budget, most items today are available in a range of prices, and this will allow you greater leeway as you plan the style in which you wish your wedding to take place. Consult anyone whose advice you feel may prove valuable, but when all is said and done, make sure that it will be the wedding you and your groom have always wanted.

# 12
# LEFTS
# AND RIGHTS

*Lydia: Uh-oh. You're right-handed and love to eat, and I'm left-handed and won't miss a meal. If I sit to your right at the reception, we may really hurt each other.*

*Lester: This is very serious, sweetheart. What are we going to do?*

*Both: (cleverly) We'll just set our table across from a mirror!*

Throughout this book and throughout your wedding planning, you will learn about the traditional side that many wedding customs take place upon. There are practical reasons, historical reasons, and sometimes no reason at all that left or right is chosen. This chapter will list the major "lefts and rights" and attempt to see a pattern, if any, in the decision of which side or which hand. At most, this will prove informative in a concise way; at least, it will make us smile as we realize that weddings should be fun, and whether the custom takes place on the "proper" side will not make a drastic difference if the celebration is a happy event for all those attending. These decisions of left or right are often simple adjustments that can be a part of your wedding planning from the beginning and should not cause any difficult or time-consuming scheming. They are usually done for practical reasons, and if not, only the strictest authority on historical etiquette will probably notice a change if you and your groom plan to make one. Let's start with the rights:

*The groom's family and friends sit on the right side of the aisle at the ceremony.*

*The ushers offer each female guest their right arm as they escort her to her seat.*

*The bride walks down the aisle on her father's right.*

*During the wedding ceremony, the bride wears her engagement ring on her right hand.*

*In a military wedding, bridesmaids walk to the right of the ushers.*

*In the receiving line, the bride stands to the groom's right.*

*At the bridal table at the reception, the bride is seated at the groom's right.*

*At the parent's table at the reception, the groom's father sits to the right of the bride's mother, and the groom's mother sits to the right of the bride's father.*

*At the cake cutting, the bride stands to the groom's right.*

*At the bachelor dinner, the best man is seated at the groom's right.*

Now for the lefts:

*The bride's family and friends sit on the left side of the aisle at the ceremony.*

*The men of the wedding party wear their boutonnieres on their left lapels.*

*The older bride and her attendants stand to the left at a double wedding.*

*The bride and groom wear their wedding rings on their left hands.*

*In the receiving line, if the groom is in uniform, the bride stands to his left.*

If we wish to analyze these requirements, we may start with practicalities. A bridesmaid walks to the right in a military wedding because her partner wears his sword on his left if he is in full uniform. The problem that could arise, what with sharp swords and soft fabrics, is evident. The bride switches her engagement ring to her right hand for the wedding ceremony because a wedding ring is about to be placed on her left. If the bride walks to her father's right, he can easily return to his pew on the left side of the church without stepping over her dress and train. The gentlemen wear their boutonnieres on their left lapels so they won't be crushed when dancing.

Next, let's consider tradition. It is believed that the vein in the third finger of the left hand leads directly to the heart, hence the choice of the left hand for the wedding band. The ultimate in traditional thinking seems to have been handed down in all of the requirements for seating. There was a time when all children were trained to do everything—from writing to eating—with the right hand. The right side was considered the stronger and more dominant one. So, to avoid a collision of elbows, people of prominence were seated to the right at the wedding festivities.

If we take a count, we will see that the rights outnumber the lefts, so if you are in doubt, the odds are in your favor to go with the right. Your best bet, however, is to determine if any physical problems or adjustments are required for the comfort of you and your guests. If you switch a left to the right or vice versa, do so with forethought and consideration, inform the necessary parties, and enjoy yourselves in the *middle* of all of this celebration!

# 13
# MUSIC

*Maxine: Mel was the only man I'd ever loved who was tone-deaf.*

*Mel: But I really wanted to enjoy the music at our wedding.*

*Both: (in rhythm) We decided we only needed a drummer.*

"If music be the food of love," someone's got to do the cooking. Music can be the single most important element of your reception party, creating mood and atmosphere, and it can be the framework for your entire wedding ceremony. It is a universal language that can conjure up the emotions of even the most serious individual in listening range, and it is a language that should be spoken with great clarity for all your guests, regardless of age or temperament. It should also be an expression of your feelings and those of your groom, so take care that the choice of the music for both your ceremony and your reception is a task that you both share. Advice may come from all quarters, but listen and sample various selections of different kinds of music and let your own good taste be your guide. You will have two decisions to make: the music you want and the musicians you want to play it.

Let us begin with the music for your wedding ceremony. If you hire instrumentalists, be they the church's regular musicians, students of music, or professional, full-time performers, some amount of payment will be expected. Some churches require that you use their musicians if you wish to use their instruments, usually an organ, piano, or other type of keyboard. Check with your clergy member about this, as well as about rules pertaining to the choice of music permitted during your ceremony. Often, nonreligious selections must be approved by the clergy member prior to the ceremony. Most church musicians have a set fee for particular services. If you have friends who will provide the music for you, obtain the officiator's permission, plan to include them in your rehearsal and at your rehearsal dinner, and give them a gift to express your thanks. When you engage any musicians, ask for suggestions on musical selections; there are many beautiful melodies you might not be familiar with that they would know from prior experience at weddings. Whether the musicians are friends or hired professionals, have them play and sing the music you have chosen about two weeks before your wedding in case there need to be any changes made. You will need to choose a specific piece for the processional and one for the recessional, usually called *marches* in the liturgical terminology. The music at the location of your wedding should start fifteen to thirty minutes prior to the ceremony, usually the time that the first guests begin to arrive. Some clergy members will permit your secular choices of music to be performed at this time. You should plan the order of songs just as you plan the order of your ceremony, and you may even wish to use certain songs as cues for what will be coming next in the progression. The music that is played before the ceremony could end with a special song for the bride's mother, as she is the last person to be seated before the ceremony begins. A special song might be selected to follow the exchange of vows or to be included in biblical readings; consider each component of your ceremony as a special link and this will aid you in selecting the music that will entice and dramatize those links.

Your musicians, whether professionals or personal friends, should definitely attend the wedding rehearsal. Even if they do not perform the music in its entirety, they should play the beginning and end of each accompaniment so all of the participants will be aware of which pieces will be performed and where they will fall in the ceremonial scheme.

Your reception music will set the tone for the festivities and should begin at the same hour that the reception itself is scheduled to commence. Enjoyable music will make your receiving line move along at a good pace and will provide a cheerful, enjoyable form of entertainment for guests as they wait to go through the line. There are many questions that you should ask before engaging a band or orchestra, and do examine all of the possible forms of musical entertainment available to you. With the development of modern electronic equipment, you can find a musician who is a one-man band, who can produce the sound of a trio or a quartet with the use of synthesizers, taped rhythm sections, and other special attachments to a keyboard or guitar. You may choose a jazz trio, a classical quartet, a five- to eight-piece band, a large orchestra. Determine if you want dancing to be a primary activity at the reception, and try to hear the group you are considering at another booking, preferably at another wedding reception. Inquire if your local musicians' union will limit who may perform in the hall where you will hold your reception. Decide if you will want the leader of the group to act as master of ceremonies, where and when you will want specific announcements and musical fanfares, and whether you will want members of the group to sing. Write out the number you will want for the first dance, as well as any other specific requests. Find out what the musicians will wear, whether you will have continuous music or if the band will take hourly breaks (if you wish to have continuous music, you may need to hire an additional pianist or enlist the aid of a talented friend), and how the rate will be computed: on an hourly basis or on a fee basis, what the overtime rate would be, whether you will be charged for any portion of an hour or only whole hours. Most groups are paid upon completion of the job, by check, but make these arrangements in advance. Find out exactly who your leader will be, because often one person's name is used as a general title for all orchestras booked from one office; you will wish to meet with the leader who will handle your reception before the party. It is also wise to know whether this is the first of two jobs for a band in any given day, or if your reception is the second or third the band will play. Make your reservation for time well in advance, especially if you suspect your reception might run longer than originally planned. By the same token, the band can also provide a comfortable ending to the festivities, playing a special last dance and thereby producing a signal for the guests to depart. Get a written contract for the musical entertainment, which stipulates the hours the group will play, the amount to be charged, the name of the leader, the exact number of musicians, the method of payment, and any other special items that may be required. If the band will use a piano or keyboard located at the reception site, make sure the instrument is tuned. This is also true for any instruments at the church. Order food and drink for the musicians and check that there will be a comfortable place for them to eat. You might also check to see if they will have need of a dressing room and that their clothing, musical equipment cases, and the like are secure while they are performing. Most musicians are very aware of the importance of this, and hold proper insurance, but it would be a nice gesture on your part to make that extra effort.

If you decide that you do not want to spend a large amount on entertainment, consider records, tapes, or the services of entertainment companies that provide a disc jockey and phonographic equipment. These organizations employ trained personnel who will act as emcee and technician for the record players and sound systems. Look under "Entertainment" in your telephone book.

You will be surprised at the range of prices available to you for music for your wedding and your reception. Your primary concern should be to engage the best possible quality for your budget. Music is often the element of your wedding that you and your guests will recall with fond memories; it is an intangible item that creates an aura of expression often greater than the spoken word.

# 14
# NAMES
# AND ADDRESSES—
# YOUR WEDDING
# INVITATIONS

*Naomi: Looking back, we really had only one major problem when we planned our wedding for five hundred guests.*

*Norman: Yeah. And it was a nice mail carrier that got us out of that pinch. Remember the day he stopped by with a mail sack just for us?*

*Both: (fondly recalling) We'd forgotten the postage.*

There was once a time when "Hear ye, hear ye," bellowed through the town square, would serve as bidding for guests to come to a wedding celebration. That era is gone, and since guests may live miles and miles away, the U.S.

mail service is today's bearer of such callings. Not only do written invitations provide the information of time and hour for the wedding, but they are keepsakes that are often framed or placed in albums and treasured as fond mementos.

You will be amazed at the variety of invitations available to you, and you will probably be besieged by mail-order companies that will send you their catalogs the moment your engagement is announced. The variety extends beyond these catalogs and the services offered by your local printer, so do some shopping before you decide on the invitation you wish to send. You may decide that your guest list is small enough for you or close relatives to write invitations by hand; you may choose to engage the services of a calligrapher; you may feel that your guest list is large enough to warrant the services of a printer or engraver. The choice is yours, and as in all facets of your wedding, do not be intimidated by your printer or anyone else who claims that there is only one way to word your invitation or have the type set. The options are yours, so let a touch of creativity and your fine taste lead the way. Here are the traditional guidelines, which will be valuable as you decide exactly how you wish to handle the creation and sending of your invitations. Invitations are a personal expression of your desire for friends and relatives to share in the happiness of your wedding festivities. You will certainly want those people to have all the necessary information—where and when the wedding will take place, and to whom they may address their acceptance. No matter how beautiful the pink paper or how lush the embossed flowers, what's essential is this information, expressed clearly and concisely.

Choose a printer or a distinguished stationer you can trust and whose samples appeal to you. A knowledgeable printer will provide a wealth of information, including the latest printing techniques, the prices for paper, and the variety in stationery and invitations available through his or her facilities. Traditionally, a formal wedding invitation is engraved on the top half of a piece of paper which has been folded in half. The paper is usually white or ivory, and the invitation is inserted in an inner, ungummed envelope upon which the full name of the guest is handwritten, and this envelope is then placed in an outer envelope which is addressed by hand, stamped and mailed. The engraving is protected by a piece of loose tissue paper, but this paper need not be left in place and sent with the invitation. It has been placed on the engraving by the printer because often the ink is not completely dried. In the past, it was sent to the guest. Today the tissue is used to prevent smudges during the engraving process; with modern printing methods, the invitations should be completely dry by the time they are delivered to you for addressing. There are many different sizes of formal invitations: a 5½- by 7½-inch invitation is usually folded a second time; a 4½- by 5¾-inch one fits the envelope as is. A return address may be printed or blindly embossed (raised letters engraved with no ink) on the back flap of the envelope or in the upper left-hand corner so that any undelivered invitations will be returned to you. The U. S. Post Office prefers that the return address be printed on the face of the envelope. Engraving is the customary form of lettering, but it may be too opulent for your budget, and another process called thermography looks almost like engraving. The only detectable difference is that you will not feel the printing if you run your finger over the back of the printed side of the invitation. The greater the number of invitations that you order, the less will be the price per copy; most printers and engravers do have minimum requirements for each price range. Even though custom calls for the two envelopes, your ecological sense may tell you to eliminate one, and this is quite satisfactory.

There are many different situations in the sponsoring

of weddings, and each can be tastefully expressed on a formal invitation. If the parents of the bride are divorced but are sponsoring the wedding together, both names may appear on the invitation. The mother of the bride can use her first name and her new surname if she has remarried. She may use her first name rather than her maiden name if she has not remarried, and the invitation would simply read: "Ms. (or Mrs.) Jane Smith and Mr. John Smith." If the bride's family and the groom's family are sharing expenses, all four names may be included on the invitation. If the wedding is being sponsored by the bride and groom along with their parents, the invitation may read "We join our parents" before the parents' names are stated. In this case the invitation would be expressed in the first person—"at our marriage," or "as we exchange marriage vows." If the bride and groom are sponsoring the wedding themselves, the wording may be "the honour of your presence is requested at the marriage of," or it may be written in the first person. If the parents are divorced, the mother of the bride may sponsor the wedding and her father may host the reception. He would send invitations in his name. If the mother of the bride is sponsoring the entire celebration, she would use her name alone as sponsor. If the mother of the bride and her new husband are sponsoring the wedding, the invitation may include both names as "Mr. and Mrs.," and the phrase "at the marriage of her daughter." If one of the parents of the bride is deceased, the other parent may sponsor alone and state, "Mr. John Smith (or Mrs. John Smith) requests the honour of your presence at the marriage of his (or her) daughter." If a relative of the bride sponsors the wedding, the invitation may include statement of the relationship, e.g., "at the wedding of her sister." If someone other than a relative sponsors the wedding, the use of Miss or Ms. before the bride's name would indicate that there is no blood relationship.

The only abbreviations included in the traditional invitation are *Mr., Mrs., Ms.,* or *Dr.* (Miss is not an abbreviation and is accepted.) No nicknames or initials are used, and all names are written in full. The first and middle names of the bride are printed directly below the phrase "their daughter" when the bride's parents are sponsoring the wedding, but if you find it more pleasing to the eye to balance your name with your groom's, you may include your last name. Including the bride's middle name is optional.

For a ceremony that will take place in a church or house of religious worship, the phrase "the honour of your presence is requested" is used. For a reception invitation or for a ceremony that will not take place in a church, the phrase "the pleasure of your company" is included. A formal request for acceptance to a reception may be included in the lower left-hand corner with the abbreviation of the French phrase *Respondez, s'il vous plaît,* R.S.V.P., or with the phrase "The favour of a reply is requested." Note that traditionally, the British spellings of *favour* and *honour* are used in formal invitations.

It used to be considered in bad taste to include a reply card in a wedding invitation; this sort of card was used for business functions rather than events that were social in nature, and anyone who was formally invited to a wedding was expected to have the decency and good manners to formally respond. Times have changed. It is perfectly acceptable to include a response card and a stamped return envelope so your guests may answer your invitation with haste. These cards are easier to handle than a variety of different sizes of stationery, and can be included as part of your filing system. Although some people consider these cards impersonal, your guests know you well enough to understand that you have included the response card to encourage their attendance on the big day. The date of the wedding is written out and the time is indicated by "o'clock" or "half after." The phrase "in the afternoon," "in the evening," or "in the morning" may also be included. The year need not be stated. Numbers are written out, although it is acceptable to use numerals if the address of the house or street is three digits or more. The state is included and written out in full unless the city is so large that there could be no mistake. If all your guests are invited to both the wedding and the reception, you may add "and afterward," with the location of the reception to your invitation. You may choose to include a separate invitation to the reception.

Here is an example of a formal wedding invitation:

> *Mr. and Mrs. John Smith*
> *request the honour of your presence*
> *at the marriage of their daughter*
> *Mary*
> *to*
> *Mr. Robert Alan Jones*
> *on Saturday, the thirty-first of January*
> *(one thousand nine hundred and eight-one—optional)*
> *at five o'clock (in the afternoon—optional)*
> *Saint Timothy's Church*
> *Ambler, Pennsylvania*

Variations are up to you.

Wedding invitations may be sent four weeks in advance of the wedding date, and should never arrive less than two weeks ahead. This means ordering your invitations at least eight to twelve weeks before this mailing date. Check with your printer for the guaranteed date of delivery and order accordingly. When ordering the number of invitations you will need, include one for each unmarried adult, one for each married couple, one for each couple living together (this is acceptable; include both names and use the same form of address you would for a married couple in which the wife has retained her maiden name), and one for each young adult over the age of thirteen to fifteen (use your discretion, you are probably familiar with the family situations of these teenagers). Plan to order a few extras for keepsakes and mementos.

Ask your printer to have the envelopes delivered early so you can begin to address them while you wait for the invitations to be completed. This will give you some extra time to do the addressing, which is done by hand. Black or dark blue ink is used to address the invitations; it is attractive to match the color of your printing if possible. The phrase "and family" need not be used; address the outer envelope to the parents, and include each of the children's first names under the parents' names on the inner envelope. List the children in order of their ages. Write out the word "and" between titles, such as "Dr. and Mrs.," as well as most numbers, with the exception of house numbers or streets that are three digits or more, e.g., 110 Street. In the past, no abbreviations, including Mr. and Ms., were used. Every city and state were written out completely. If you find that you do not have the time to devote to this lengthy type of addressing, feel free to abbreviate. The post office personnel are far more concerned with Zip codes (which should be included) than with the spelling of the state they work in. It is visually pleasing to choose a stamp that is commemorative, if you so desire. Have an invitation with all its enclosures weighed at the post office before you purchase or affix any stamps. The invitations should be sent by first-class mail, which guarantees the return of undeliverable mail, and should an invitation be returned due to an incorrect address, do not hesitate to telephone the guest immediately. This also holds true if you have, by mistake, omitted a guest from your invitation list. The telephone, and sincere apologies expressed in your own voice, work wonders in these cases.

The inside envelope only needs the titles and the

surname, e.g., Mr. and Mrs. Smith, and it should be addressed in the same hand as its outer envelope. The inner envelope should be placed in the outer with the front of the inner facing the back of the outer so that names on the inner are read immediately. The invitation itself is placed in the inner envelope with the folded edge down and with the engraving facing the back of the envelope. As confusing as these two previous sentences may sound, what is really suggested is that the invitations be sent in a fashion that is easiest for quick reading.

You may decide that you would like to hire a calligrapher to address your invitations for you. This fancy type of script writing is done by hand, and most calligraphers charge per invitation. Make sure that you supply the artist with an accurate listing of all your guests, and state exactly how you wish their invitations to read. The Yellow Pages of your phone book, a local art school, or a printing and engraving establishment can usually supply you with the names of calligraphers.

There are other ways to extend your invitations than the formal manner described above. You may decide to handwrite your invitations or hire an artist or calligrapher to do so, especially if your wedding is small, fifty guests or less, and you have decided on an informal affair. If you choose to write your own, they may be done on any size and color of paper that you like, and you may use the form of a short personal note. This note may be written in the first person, and may be from either yourself, your parents, or you and your groom, or some may be from your groom himself to his personal friends. The note can start off with "Dear" and go from there. It should include the important details of time and place and can easily ask for a reply. You might even include your invitation in the newspaper announcement of your engagement, if the journal permits it, by adding the phrase "No invitations are being sent, but all friends and relatives are invited to attend the wedding." Needless to say, this is only done in very small towns and villages, where most, if not all, of the community members know one another. And finally, if you choose to have a wedding that is completely private, you may wish to include a statement to that effect in the newspaper announcement of your engagement. Obviously, you would withhold all pertinent information of time and place of the ceremony.

The only time you should not expect a reply from your invited guests is when you invite them to the ceremony only, not to a reception. Otherwise, an invitation to a wedding celebration should be answered as quickly as possible, and a short note or a formal reply should be on its way to the sponsors of the wedding. Either type of reply is acceptable, as long as your guests do notify you of either their acceptance or their regrets that they cannot attend. A formal reply is written by hand in the same language as the formal invitation itself. This means using the third person voicing and repeating the words of the invitation, e.g., your guest's name "accepts with pleasure the kind invitation of (your sponsors') for" the event, date, and time of the festivities. If they must decline the invitation they simply write "regret that they are unable to accept the kind invitation for" and state the event. The quickest and easiest method of reply is the return of an enclosed response card; these cards include a space for the guest's name and a blank to fill in whether they will or will not attend. Hopefully, your guests will understand that a reply to your invitation is not just a formality, but a necessity if you are to make your plans for the reception. If you have not heard from some of your guests, and your deadline is approaching, pick up the telephone and call them directly.

When some, but not all, of your guests will be invited to the reception, a separate reception card should be used. This card is usually exactly half the size of the invitation and is identical in type, printing, and paper stock. Like the invitation, it will be delivered to you with a protective tissue, which need not be included in the envelope with the invitation. If a meal is to be served at the reception, you may wish to note this on the invitation by stating the word *dinner* or *luncheon* after the word *reception*. You may decide to limit the number of guests at the ceremony and have a large number of people at the reception. In this case, the larger invitation would be used for the reception and the smaller for the wedding invitation. The bride's first name and the groom's first and last names would be joined by the word "and." The phrase "pleasure of your company" would be used.

Here is an example:

> *Mr. and Mrs. James Backman*
> *request the pleasure of your company*
> *at the wedding reception of their daughter*
> *Marie*
> *and*
> *Mr. David John Connor*
> *Saturday, the twentieth of June*
> *at five o'clock*
> *The Victorian Manor*
> *1000 Butler Road*
> *Ambler, Pennsylvania*

When a wedding is extremely large, or if the persons being married are celebrities of any sort, church cards are issued with the invitation. They are printed on the same paper and in the same style as the invitation, and they should read "please present this card," and should include the date and location of the wedding. Ushers should be instructed to only permit persons who are carrying these cards to enter the church. There is another type of card called a pew card, which is used to guarantee particular seating, usually up front, to certain relatives and friends.

These cards may be printed or may be handwritten on your informal stationery or that of your mother's. The card may include the phrase "bride's reserved section" or "groom's reserved section," or a more traditional phrase, "within the ribbons," may be used. These cards should be sent after acceptances are received (you may wish to make a specific seating plan), and ushers should be instructed where guests carrying these cards are to be directed to sit.

If you find it necessary to include a map to your ceremony and reception, check with the establishment where your reception will be held, because they may supply you with a map. If not, have a map drawn and printed or copied, not engraved. You can include the map right in the invitation; there is no need to waste postage and paper by sending them under separate cover. If you decide to send at-home cards, they may be included in the invitation as well; they are a convenience to friends and relatives if you will be moving to a city other than your hometown. The card should include your new names or the way you will state your name after marriage, the new address with Zip code, and the phrase "at home after" and a specific date. If you have established your new residence during your engagement period or prior to your marriage, simply do not include a date or the word *after*. At-home cards may be sent after the wedding, or you may accomplish the same purpose by using stationery with your new address to send thank-you notes for gifts. If you are having stationery monogrammed, there are a variety of different styles and arrangements of initials. The blocks used for engraving may be used for many years and on various kinds of paper, so choose a style that you will enjoy for a long period of time.

A wedding announcement is sent after the ceremony has taken place, and is a nice way of letting friends and acquaintances who were not invited to the wedding know of your new status. Announcements are never sent to guests who were invited to the wedding or reception; they may be sent after any type of wedding, including civil ceremonies or elopements. Check with your stationer for samples of announcements; they are very similar in size and form to wedding invitations. An average announcement would read: "Mr. and Mrs. John Smith have the honor of announcing the marriage of their daughter, Amy, to Mr. Robert Jones." The date and the year of marriage are included, and usually the location and church name are stated. If the ceremony was a civil one, or if the couple eloped, only the city and state need be included. The announcement may be made by the parents of the bride, or any of the situations listed above for formal invitations may exist. Here is an example of an announcement sent by divorced parents:

*Mrs. T. Robert Kramer*
*and*
*Mr. William Clinton*
*announce the marriage*
*of their daughter*
*Margie Clinton*
*to*
*Dwight Conway, Jr.*
*on Saturday, the twenty-first of June*
*Nineteen hundred and eighty*
*Apple Creek Farm*
*Old Lyme, Connecticut*

In any of these cases, the parties making the announcement would list their names in the same fashion as would the sponsors of a wedding for which a formal invitation is sent. A recipient of a wedding announcement is not obligated to send a gift or even to forward acknowledgment of receipt of the announcement. It is simply a gracious gesture to inform friends, relatives, and often business associates that the wedding has taken place. You may enclose an at-home card with the announcement.

In today's modern society, any situation can be tastefully expressed in print. Perhaps you are a widow; perhaps you have been divorced. In either of these situations, you may be remarrying and you may be sponsoring your own wedding; or you may be accepting the kindness of your parents, who wish to sponsor it for you. Your parents may be divorced, your groom's parents may be divorced, each one may have married again or married twice again. Whatever your situation, take the names and titles of the persons involved as they are used on a day-to-day basis, combine them with yours (whether you use your maiden name, your former married surname, or any other), and write the wording of your invitation in the manner in which your dear friends and relatives know you and care for you. It is your official request that they join you for an event that is very important. An invitation to attend a marriage should be cause for celebration, and each and every word included in it should contribute to the feeling of happiness that will be shared.

# 15
# OFFICIATOR

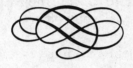

*O*live: *Oscar, Father O'Brien says this could be a first.*

*O*scar: *Rabbi Omar says he'll try anything once.*

*B*oth: *So we'll all meet at the Presbyterian Chapel at twelve noon. . . .*

A person who *officiates* can be anyone from a high priest to an umpire. It is a term which means, simply, to perform a ceremony or administer rules in an official capacity. You will need someone to officiate at your marriage, be it a priest, minister, rabbi, or a judge, and his or her task will be to act as the celebrant of your wedding ceremony. The officiator will carry out the necessary functions of your service, but will not marry you . . . only you and your groom can do that. It seems like a minor distinction, but it is the misunderstanding of this fact that leads to ceremonies which you've heard a thousand times before—"*do you* take, *do you* promise, until death *do you* part"—which *do not* necessarily express the vows which will signify a union for life. Even if you choose to pronounce the classical vows, and they are certainly quite valid, it is important to comprehend their meaning and willingly accept their public recitation. For it is the two of you who answer to the marriage vows; your officiate is posing the questions.

Do not leave your wedding ceremony to chance. Plan to meet with the officiator you have chosen well before your marriage day and discuss all the ceremonial details. In the case of most religious weddings, you will make all arrangements for the use of the church with the minister or priest who will act as officiator for your marriage. Start with these basic questions: Is this particular clergy member available on the day and at the time that you wish to be married? Will the church itself be suitable for the kind of wedding you've planned? Can the rehearsal be scheduled at a convenient time for all involved? Does the church enforce any special regulations regarding decorations, flowers, mode of dress, photography? Are there an organ and organist available and are their use mandatory? Will the readings, prayers, vows, sermons, and speeches that you and your groom choose need to be approved by the officiator? Will they be approved? Most importantly, is this person willing to officiate *and* is this the person that you wish to officiate? Finally, what fees will be charged? With the exception of the questions that specifically relate to the church itself, you will make the same inquiries if you wish to have your clergy member officiate at any other location. You may decide that even if neither you nor your groom have a particular religious affiliation, you wish to be married in a church setting. You may have a friend or relation who is a member of a religious order whom you would like to ask to officiate. If either of these situations arise, you will need to find out if that clergy member will be allowed to perform the ceremony outside of his or her own parish or church, and if you will be permitted to be married in a church of which you are not a member. These circumstances are not unusual, and the majority of religious officiators are willing to work with you on arrangements of this nature. Do plan well in advance.

If you will have a civil ceremony, plans must also be made in advance, especially if your wedding will be held anywhere other than a judge's chambers. With an officiator, religious or civil, you will want to discuss the contents of the ceremony itself, make arrangements for the officiator to attend the rehearsal, and be sure that he or she is given clear and concise directions to the location of the wedding.

The clergy member or judge should be paid the necessary fee immediately following the ceremony, although some churches request that the "offering" be presented on the evening of the rehearsal. It is also customary to give a small gratuity to altar boys or sextons. At a formal wedding, the best man assumes the duty of making sure the officiator receives the fee; a check or cash (it's a nice touch to use brand-new bills for any service which is paid for in cash) is placed in a sealed envelope addressed with the officiator's name. Most clergy members or judges will not be shy about discussing fees, but feel free to ask about amounts and if a check or cash is preferred.

If everyone except you, your groom, his best man, and your maid of honor left the room, the only person you would need to recognize your wedding as legal would be your officiator. This does not mean that that person should be a mechanical member of the wedding. Your officiator might just be an acquaintance or might become a friend for life, but it should be a person who considers your wishes, a person you respect, and a person who will share in your joy, even if the only words spoken are in an official capacity.

# 16
# PARTIES
# AND SHOWERS

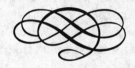

*Priscilla: We had twelve showers, six cocktail parties, four luncheons, eight dinners.*

*Perry: Three dances, five brunches, and two picnics.*

*Both: One night, we forgot to go.*

What has guests, gifts, food, drink, is often a surprise, usually happens before a wedding, and sounds like rain? The answer is the showers and parties that your friends and family will give in honor of your marriage. You may find yourself inundated with celebrations that you will *have* to attend because they will all be for you and your groom. Many of these affairs will have a singular purpose: gift giving to help you and your groom outfit your new home. The cause of celebration may be announcement of your intent to marry. Some of this merrymaking will be the reconfirmation of friendships, the getting together of your bridesmaids or his ushers to share a meal and lots of tradition. And still other of these occasions will be your way of thanking guests for traveling many miles to be with you at your wedding and thanking your attendants for their concern and participation in all the planning of the event, especially the rehearsal of the actual ceremony.

There are certain types of parties that are traditional, and they will be described in the order in which they usually occur. However, there are no laws governing styles and numbers of parties to be celebrated, so if you would rather have a midnight supper instead of a luncheon, feel free to do so. And if you find that you have not one moment remaining in your schedule before your wedding, suggest that your friend who wishes to give a barbecue in your honor do so after your honeymoon. (It's fun to have a wedding-picture party a few months after your wedding, once everyone has returned to a normal routine.) Since you and your groom must be in attendance at all these events, because the parties are being given for you, you are entitled to leave first. This is quite proper and gives you the opportunity to control, to a certain extent, the length of the festivities. The other area of control that will often fall into your hands will be the guest list; if a prospective hostess asks you to provide her with a list of people you would like to attend a gathering, do so immediately. Provide her with the list of names, addresses, and phone numbers, and note your relationship to the person (second cousin, secretary, supervisor, best friend) if the hostess has never met the invitee. Ask exactly how many guests you should list, and plan to stay within the number given. Also, remember the power of suggestion, since your friends and family members may be planning a surprise party, but genuinely wish to make you happy. If there is a certain gift you need, or a certain type of party you would like to celebrate, or a specific cuisine you simply can't eat, tell close relatives and friends, and hint that you would appreciate their spreading the word. This is best exemplified by the desire for gifts of money—a perfectly reasonable request, but one that many people will not assume if you do not let them know.

### Engagement Parties

An engagement party is given by the bride-to-be's family if the occasion is the actual announcement of marriage. However, once your engagement has been announced, friends or relatives of the bride or groom may wish to give a party to celebrate the upcoming wedding, or you may wish to give a party that will give all of your attendants a chance to get to know one another if they have never met. If the festivities are being planned by your parents to make the first official announcement of your engagement, your invitations will not state this, although most of your friends will assume the happy news. No gifts should be expected for this type of celebration. It has become customary that midway through an engagement party, be it a full dinner or just champagne cocktails and hor d'oeuvres, the father of the bride proposes a toast to you and your fiancé and states your intention to be married. After he has made the announcement, your fiancé may express thanks by returning another toast of his own. An engagement party is by no means obligatory, but can be very enjoyable if the host and hostess feel comfortable and share their enjoyment with their guests. This is true of all festive affairs—a happy host makes guests feel relaxed and provides the essential ingredients for making any of these prewedding parties memorable.

## Showers

There is one theme that is consistent for all showers: The purpose of the get-together is to give gifts. Traditionally, showers were only given for the bride; today joint showers are very common, and a prewedding party for male and female guests can still be considered a shower and still serve the same purpose. Almost any gift that is given for the newlyweds' household is used by both bride and groom and even a beautiful negligee or a rich after-shave cologne can be enjoyed by both in these liberated times! Showers are given by anyone except members of the immediate families of the bride or groom, unless the maid of honor is a relative of the bride. If she chooses to host a shower, the family rule does not apply. Friends and relatives are invited to a shower for the bride, but people who do not know her—even though they may attend the wedding—are not invited. Traditionally, all your attendants should be invited to every shower, but since all guests are expected to bring a gift to a shower, it is wise of you to see that guests lists are different if many showers are scheduled. If your bridesmaids do attend more than one shower, request that they limit their gift purchases to moderate amounts, or attempt to make it clear that you do not expect lavish gifts ten times over. The best solution to this problem is to let it be known that one general shower, rather than many smaller ones, is perfectly acceptable to you. You can usually get any or all of these types of messages through to your friends and acquaintances by keeping your mother, your maid of honor, and your fiancé's mother informed of your personal feelings about these matters, for they are the ones who are likely to be consulted by well-meaning friends. Showers may be planned for almost any time of day, and it's fun to vary from the typical afternoon party and consider a brunch or an early evening potluck supper. The hostess may decide to designate a specific gift theme for the party, and here's where your information sources (your mother and maid of honor) can best serve you. If you have every possible item ever designed for kitchen use, the last thing you'll need is a culinary shower. However, make sure the category you choose has a wide range of prices and does not imply only costly presents. Any guest who attends a shower will probably attend the wedding, so their gift giving will happen at least twice. The actual opening of gifts takes place at the shower and is usually the primary entertainment of the hour. As you open each gift, thank the giver immediately, and although a thank-you note is not obligatory, it is a nice gesture on your part that reemphasizes your appreciation in a very personal way. It is obligatory to send notes of thanks for gifts that are received from persons who could not attend the shower, and also to your host and hostess. You may receive joint gifts; each person should be thanked separately. Showers are almost always informal, and along with the giving of gifts, provide a time for visiting, conversation, and usually some delicious eating for all in attendance.

### Bridesmaids' Luncheon

The bridesmaids' luncheon is usually given by the bride, but may be given by the attendants themselves or by a relative of the bride. And the bridesmaids' luncheon need not be a luncheon. It may be a small dinner party, a late breakfast after the final fitting of the bridesmaids' dresses, or an evening dessert party. This is a good time to give your thank-you gifts to your maid of honor and bridesmaids, and this get-together provides a chance for you to be with your attendants in a relaxed atmosphere a few days before the wedding. There is an old tradition often upheld at this affair: a small ring is baked into the cake that is served for dessert (usually pink ladies' cake), and the person who receives the piece with the ring is the one who will be married next. All of your attendants, your mother, and your fiancé's mother should be invited to this occasion. You might even schedule it at the same time that your groom's bachelor dinner will be held.

### Bachelor's Dinner

We've all heard stories about wild bachelor dinners that provide a fantastic last fling for the groom before he ties the knot. Left to his own devices, your groom's best man can probably decide what his friend would enjoy the most and plan to give the party with the other attendants, or your groom can host this event himself. Like the bridesmaids' lunchon, this party is a chance for your groom to relax with his friends before the wedding day, and is also a good time for him to distribute his thank-you gifts. The tradition that holds for the bachelor's party is that at the end of the party, the groom proposes a champagne toast to his bride, after which all of the ushers smash their glasses so that the glass may serve no other, less worthy purpose. This tradition requires that your groom plan in advance to have extra glasses available. No matter what type of party is planned to celebrate the end of your groom's bachelor-hood, request that it be held any time other than the night before the wedding. If you schedule your bridesmaids' party at the same time, you can make it just as wild as the bachelor's dinner, and perhaps you can all get together for a nightcap at the end of the evening!

### Rehearsal Dinner

Even if you and your groom dislike all kinds of parties and showers, the rehearsal dinner is one event that is *almost* a necessity, not just to provide some relaxation and suste-nance, but to allow for any last-minute discussions and arrangements that need to be made between you and members of your wedding party just prior to the actual wedding. The rehearsal dinner is usually held immediately after the rehearsal is completed, and it is hosted by the groom's parents. However, your family may host this party or share the responsibilities. If the groom's parents are traveling a long distance, you may suggest restaurants of various types that would be suitable for the rehearsal dinner and provide your future mother-in-law with addresses and telephone numbers of the restaurants so she can make all the necessary arrangements in advance. A restaurant that is convenient to reach from the location of the church is always preferable. You and your parents, your groom and his parents, all of your attendants and their husbands and wives, the ceremony officiator and spouse, and the parents of any young children who will be members of your wedding party are invited to the rehearsal dinner. It may be too late in the evening for the children themselves to attend. You might also extend an invitation to the musicians and soloists who attended the rehearsal. Sometimes, if you and your family are sharing hosting the rehearsal dinner, you may wish to invite out-of-town guests who have arrived for the wedding, especially if it is held the night before a morning or early afternoon wedding. If you do need to schedule this way, arrange to have the rehearsal and dinner at an hour that will be early enough to allow everyone a good night's rest before the big day. You may decide to give your thank-you gifts to your attendants at the rehearsal dinner. The groom's father is usually the person who makes the toast at this occasion. It is wise to send an invitational reminder to all the guests that will provide them with written details about time and place of the rehearsal dinner, although this information may be telephoned. The rehearsal dinner need not be formal and may be held at the home of either the groom's family, the bride's family or a relative of either. It is often one of the most comfortable and most pleasant parties of all, since the weeks of planning are successfully coming to a close, and what better way to spend the evening before your wedding than with your husband-to-be and your dearest friends and relatives?

## *Parties After the Wedding*

If your wedding is scheduled at a time that will mean guests from out of town or relatives who have traveled a great distance will not return to their homes until the next day, it is a lovely gesture to hold a breakfast or brunch on the day after the wedding, before they start their journeys. Any member of either family or a close friend may host an event of this nature, and this is one party that you will not be expected to attend. You and your groom will probably have departed on your wedding trip and be miles away by the time these people gather.

If your groom's parents have other friends whom they were not able to invite to the reception because of limited places, they may decide to give a party or a second reception after you return from your honeymoon, or even a few months after the official wedding day for as many guests as they may wish to invite.

Unless a party is specifically planned as a shower, with the exception of the reception itself, gifts should not be expected. Do not be surprised, though, if friends or distant relatives do come bearing gifts, especially in the case of the second reception. Be gracious, express your appreciation, and follow up with a written thank-you note. You need not feel obliged to open a gift immediately, except at a shower, where gift giving—the "showering" of presents upon the bride—is the purpose of the event.

The parties and showers that come with the planning of a wedding can be very time-consuming, but they can also be hours that are filled with everything from fancy regalement to good old-fashioned fun. Enjoy every moment, even if you and your groom have to make appointments with each other to be in a room that isn't filled with other people. Only good friends and loving relatives will devote the time and absorb the expense it takes to give a party in your honor, no matter how large or small. The parties that you and your groom will give are also only planned because you care about those friends and relatives that will share in the celebration of your marriage. Eat, drink, and be merry!

# 17
# QUESTIONS
# OFTEN ASKED

*Quintilla: Is there anything else you'd like to ask, Quentin?*

*Quentin: You've already answered the only important question I had.*

*Both: (shyly) Of course . . . I'll marry you!*

Here are some of the questions that are asked most frequently about weddings today. The list may include every item you've ever wondered about or might not even touch on the topic about which you have a question. If the latter is the case, feel free to address your inquiry to: Edythe Vincent, Alfred Angelo, Inc., 601 Davisville Road,

Willow Grove, Pa. 19090. She'll send you an answer quicker than you can say A, B, C!

Q. *How can we let people know that a "purse" shower, or wedding gifts of cash, are best for us?*

A. Today's bride and groom often already own many of the traditional wedding gifts by virtue of the fact that they have each maintained fully equipped homes prior to marriage. This is the reason that the finest gift for this couple is a gift of cash, no matter what the amount. The best way to let people know this is twofold: First, let your honor attendants (both the best man and the maid of honor) and both sets of parents know of your wishes, and instruct them to feel free to tell people who ask what to give that you would like money. Use the explanation above. Anyone who wishes to give you a shower will contact your close friends or relatives, so let the word out. Don't be shy. Secondly, if your friends and relatives ask you directly, do not hem and haw, just say that you would appreciate a cash gift. You might mention that you are saving for a special item (a trip around the world would be wonderful someday!) to put their minds at ease. Think about it this way. In the long run, your friends will probably be grateful that you've let them know that you wish money, because if you're "the person who has everything," you may be difficult to shop for. A gift certificate is money, a check is money, a bond is money, a basket of coins is money. Shopping is easier at a bank!

If there are special gifts you would like that are not the traditional ones, and which are not carried by a department store where you would be able to register your choices, make a list and give this to your honor attendants and parents. You can do this with great propriety, you might decide to letter it or express it in a humorous manner, and you will be much more likely to get the rolling garbage can that you really want and need.

If you do not wish to receive gifts at all, you can state

this on your invitations. By saying, "no gifts, please," there is no one who will misunderstand. If you have a favorite charity that you feel strongly about, ask that donations be made to it in your name as a wedding remembrance. Absolutely, perfectly acceptable.

*Q. I have been invited to the wedding and shower of a dear friend, but am on a very limited budget. How do I solve the gift-giving problem?*

A. If you can, choose a gift that is in two parts, and give the larger part as one gift and the smaller as another. For instance, you could give a beautiful teapot as the shower gift, and the matching cups as your wedding gift. You could purchase these as one, but divide them into two gifts. If you give a large salad bowl as one gift, you might give the matching tongs as another. Or consider giving yourself! Make a small certificate that entitles the bearers to a meal created by you after the wedding. No matter how small the gift, your friend isn't a friend if she or he judges you by the price tag on your package. It's that invaluable thought that counts.

*Q. What should guests wear to a wedding?*

A. Guests should understand the degree of formality you have chosen for your wedding from the invitation that you send. From that point on, the options are theirs. Today any color, including black or white, is acceptable for guests at a wedding. Overdressing can be just as uncomfortable as underdressing, and any guest who has a question about what should be worn should not hesitate to contact the host or hostess. Be prepared with an answer to that question, whether you want your guests to wear blue jeans or tuxedos.

*Q. Must bridesmaids dress alike, must ushers dress alike, and must there be an equal number of bridesmaids and ushers?*

A. The answer on all three counts is no. If you will need the services of more ushers than bridesmaids, or vice versa, it is acceptable to ask them to join your wedding party. If your guest list is long, you may need a good number of ushers to seat everyone in a specific amount of time; there is nothing worse than standing in line waiting to be seated to wait for a wedding to begin! If you need an extra bridesmaid to carry your train, ask her to join your party; she won't need an usher to escort her under those circumstances anyway. Moreover, if there is someone that either you or your groom wish to have as a member of the wedding, an addition to the pairs of other ushers and bridesmaids, their friendship and participation is far more important than their lack of a partner. You may decide to have the entire wedding party exit in single file, or give that extra person the "honor" of walking alone. This often happens when a flower girl or ring bearer, but not both, is in the wedding party.

You and your groom oversee the choice of attire for your attendants. If your wedding will be a happier one for you with each person dressed individually, feel free to plan this way. Just give consideration to the coordination of all the different looks. You might vary trim. You might choose different colors for the men's shirts. You might have the women wear a similar style in different colors. What's important here is that your attendants' appearance reflects the tone you and your groom have chosen for your own attire and your ceremony. There is, however, something to be said for the powerful effect similar dresses and suits can have. Consider the choruses of an exquisite ballet or grand musical, traditional tabernacle or military choirs, even sports teams and cheerleading squads! Their impact is heightened by the glorious costume that all members wear. It makes them feel proud of their position and distinguishes them from the crowd. The choice is yours, so think about the effect you'll want to produce to surround you on your wedding day.

Q. *I want a traditional, formal wedding gown with all*

*the trimmings. What are the restrictions on length of train?*

A. The first restriction is space. If your very formal wedding is being held in a country chapel, your train, quite literally, may not fit down the aisle. The second restriction is coordination with the entire mood of your wedding. Never has a dress with a train been less than formal, even if it is made of feathers and glitter to be worn in the finale of a Broadway show. Somehow, a man in casual attire standing next to a woman in a train will fade into the background. The factors that will *not* restrict the wearing of a train are time of day and number of guests. A formal wedding may be held during the day and may be planned for a small group of guests. Even if a full meal is not served, champagne and caviar can be formal fare. A train is part of the look you wish to have on your wedding day, and the look should make you feel wonderful.

*Q. Should we read every word of our ceremony at the rehearsal?*

A. Not necessarily. The actual vow taking will only happen once, so if you, your groom, and your officiator can go over that portion of the ceremony privately, it may have more meaning for you and your guests at its official moment. However, any cue words that will signal the singing of a song, the movement of attendants, the reading of a parable, or any section of the ceremony that involves persons other than you, your groom, and your officiator, should be rehearsed. This insures the smooth running of the event.

*Q. Are there any acceptable alternatives to the traditional engraved invitation?*

A. Absolutely. The only tradition that need be upheld is that the message of who, where, and when be received. By stating these facts, your choice of language and the remaining content of the invitation will imply what type of wedding you have planned. So feel free to write your invitation in paragraph form. Have the lines printed flush rather than having each one centered. Add artwork or photographs. Eliminate the inner envelope and tissue if you wish, especially if your conscience will bother you about the waste of paper. This is a fact to consider as our natural resources wane. When eliminating the tissue, make sure the ink is dry, usually a problem that does not arise with today's modern printing methods. You and your groom can abandon the formal wording and write your own invitation or announcement. If your parents are sponsoring the wedding, they might wish to express themselves in a more contemporary fashion. You may have a special statement to make or some information to impart that has never been included in a traditional wedding announcement. Consider the following:

*Stephen L. Leighton*
*and*
*Deborah C. Gregory*
*would like to announce their marriage*
*and, with her son, Jesse,*
*the coming together of a new family.*

*In their coming together*
*a new consciousness is born,*
*which, in its new and radiant life,*
*shelters and supports the growth*
*of each part.*

*The printing of this invitation was a wedding gift to the couple from Loom Press, Chapel Hill, N.C.*

As long as you pass on the vital information your guests will need, and do so with taste, your invitation need not follow any traditional requirements unless you wish it to.

*Q. Where did the ivory color for wedding dresses originate?*

A. Even though white is the most conventional color for wedding gowns today, stemming from the ancient belief that white symbolized purity and joy, the color of wedding gowns has varied throughout countries and centuries. The ancient Chinese bride wore red because it was considered a symbol of gaiety and festivity. No matter what color, early American brides often just wore their best dress, and gowns specifically designed for American marriages didn't come into popularity until 1800. When they did, a very light brown shade was the fashionable color because it was more complimentary to the bride's skin than white. The color ivory is a member of the white family and is considered a satisfactory replacement for stark white if it is more flattering to the bride's coloring and features.

*Q. How much should a wedding cost?*

A. There is no specific dollar value that should be spent. Some people spend thousands, some hundreds, some less. Statistics, which are merely averages of the numbers computed, say twenty-five hundred dollars was the average amount spent on weddings in 1980. That figure might change tomorrow and is different from yesterday. Your only guide is this: Use the dollars you wish to spend on your wedding to their optimum purchasing power. Whether this means one hundred dollars for champagne for ten or ten thousand dollars for dinner for five hundred, it matters not if those people share happily in your celebration. You can purchase any item necessary for a wedding in a wide range of prices. This includes everything from your gown (yes, a wedding dress can be pretty *and* inexpensive) to your honeymoon (you can "leave the driving to us" rather than "fly the friendly skies").

If going into debt will make you and your family miserable, don't do it for the joyous occasion of your marriage. However, if spending a large amount on your wedding will make you, your groom, and your wedding sponsors extremely happy, get out your checkbooks without hesitation.

*Q. There are certain elements of the traditional wedding that my groom, our families, and I like. May we combine them with our contemporary choices?*

A. A wedding is like a good recipe. What difference do the ingredients make if the final result is delicious? Anything that tastes wonderful usually means the right combinations in the proper amounts have been mixed and cooked to perfection. Get out your spoons, preheat the oven, and remember, you're the chef!

All kidding aside, now. If you didn't combine choices that all blend together to produce the wedding you want, you'd be making a serious mistake.

## 18
# RECEPTIONS

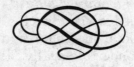

*Rose: I think it should be really unique, wonderfully special, something no one's done before.*

*Ralph: A reception that people will remember for years, that they can't wait to get to and won't want to leave.*

*Both: Mr. President, we were wondering if the Oval Office would be free on the third Saturday of June. . . .*

Your wedding reception can be a gala, a jamboree, a clambake, a picnic, a carnival, a ball, a banquet, a square dance, a medieval revelry, an outdoor spree, an indoor soiree, a sit-down dinner, a stand-up tea. Whatever you choose, it is your celebration of your wedding for your guests. It is a party with a unique purpose, the sharing of a special occasion with friends and relatives, and like any other party, every detail must be planned in advance. Many factors will influence the type of party you give, from hosting the event to paying the bills. The answers to three questions—where, when, and what—should be determined as far in advance as possible, preferably when you and your groom set a date for marriage. The larger and more formal your affair, the more planning it will take, so begin immediately to contact all the people who can offer the services you will want. Have ready all the information they will need to give you price estimates on what they can provide. This information will include: the date you wish to hold the reception (most people have a wedding reception on the same day as their wedding, but you may decide to have it later), with a second and third choice, especially during the busy wedding months of June, August, September and December; the number of people you will want to invite; the time of day you wish to have the party (remember that a reception that is not held at a commonly accepted dining hour, but is scheduled either early in the afternoon or later in the evening, means a full meal need not be served); how long you wish the party to run (the average reception lasts approximately three hours, and many reception sites rent by the hour); and the type of setting you wish to have for your festivities. Consider the proximity of the location of the hotel, restaurant, club, or hall to the place where you will be married, the amount of space you will need, whether you will want a dance floor—and most importantly, whether this location will be available on the date you wish to celebrate, since many establishments that book wedding receptions have calendars that are filled a year in advance.

Decide how much money you want to invest in this party. There are special reception packages that are at a fixed price; check if each item in these packages meets with your approval. Most caterers or restaurants will charge per person, but whatever price range you are considering, remember to add 15 to 25 percent for tax and gratuities. Don't let anything slip you by—you will be investing in food, drink, music, decorations, and service. Don't rely on one-stop shopping. Check a variety of suppliers and ask for estimates and a description of the services before deciding which one will best meet your needs. Locate caterers, musicians, and other people who have been recommended to you highly or whose reputations you feel are of the finest standards. Make appointments with these people rather than just dropping in to see them so you will have the time you personally need to ask questions and discuss your needs. The voice of experience is very valuable, and any person who is affiliated with an establishment that has planned and produced these kinds of events could be the key to smooth planning for your reception. However, do not let a restaurant owner, banquet manager, or bridal consultant force you into any decisions that you feel would not be in keeping with the type of party you wish to have. Once you decide, have all details, all costs, and all liabilities (in case you would have to cancel) put in writing. Read all contracts, even the fine print, very carefully before signing. There are some basic elements that are common to most receptions, they are described below. Alter them in any way you feel will make your reception more enjoyable, for enjoyment is the only element that is common to all receptions.

The degree of formality you will choose for your reception is completely up to you, but you will probably want it to coincide with the tone set by the wedding ceremony itself. An extremely formal reception starts with a receiving line and usually includes the partaking of a full meal, served by waiters and waitresses to guests who are seated at tables with place cards. Champagne is served for the formal toasting to the new couple, and a variety of other drinks, usually in an open-bar situation, is available to all guests throughout the reception. At an informal reception, many of the more traditional activities may be dispensed with. You may choose to eliminate the receiving line (you and your groom would still greet all of your guests as they arrive), plan a buffet meal rather than a dinner served by waiters and waitresses, and have a wine punch rather than a full bar. A reception that follows a morning ceremony and includes the noon hour might offer a meal called a wedding breakfast, but which is actually a rather elegant luncheon. An early afternoon wedding can be followed by a stand-up reception of drinks and light hors d'oeuvres; a late afternoon wedding usually leads into a reception that will include dinner. An evening wedding, at which the ceremony is held between the hours of seven and nine P.M., can include a light supper. An at-home reception can be any degree of formality, but will require the extra time it takes to plan for the rental of extra silverware, dishes, glasses, and the like, the hiring of servers and possibly a bartender, the enlisting of friends to help with preparation and serving if you choose to do the cooking yourself, menu planning and food shopping for it, and the choice of where your ceremony and where your party will take place if scheduled for the same interior space. If you decide to request the use of a friend's home for a reception rather than a rental hall, make it clear that you will take care of everything, that nothing more than your friend's generosity with the location will be expected. The number of guests greatly influences any kind of reception; 25 people at your home is a reasonable number to entertain, 250 may not be.

When it's time to plan your reception, choose your caterer wisely, for an experienced one will be able to handle every detail from appetizers to after-dinner mints. People who claim to be food and beverage experts will be great in number. A good caterer will advise you on liquor needs (often the most expensive item of any reception), will give you a wide choice of menu, and may even handle the ordering of your wedding cake if you so desire. Most caterers charge on a per-person basis and will require a minimum guarantee on number of guests. You should feel perfectly free to ask to see the caterer's equipment —including the china, silverware, and linens that will be used—and it is very wise to ask to be served the meal that you've chosen before your actual reception date. This "taste test" will avoid the discomfort of eating a food that does not appeal to you. Ask the caterer who will be in charge of your reception and plan to meet this person in advance. Most likely it will be the caterer himself, but in a large hotel or restaurant there might be a number of managerial personnel involved with your party. You want to know, who is "the boss," and meet this person, for he or she will be present for the duration of your reception. Discuss the number of people you will need to hire; a bartender is usually required for every fifty to one hundred persons, and depending on the type of meal, the number of necessary table servers will vary. A buffet setup is more simple than a sit-down dinner; a clambake means you'll need people who specialize in seafood; cake and punch might only require one waitress. Any form of food serving requires cleanup personnel.

The serving of alcoholic beverages may be handled in many different ways. You might choose to have a bar that will serve continuously throughout the party and will be stocked with a large variety of liquor, wine, and beer. This type of service is called open bar, and it means that you and your guests may drink as much as you please. The charge for this type of bar is calculated on the number of opened (not empty) bottles that remain after the festivities are over. It is very difficult to control this sort of set up, so if your budget is not inexhaustable, you should set some form of limit, either in number of hours the bartenders will serve or number of bottles that may be opened. You can instruct the bartenders to alert you when either of these numbers are reached and then you may decide if you wish to increase your order or close the bar. You might opt for a limited bar, which means you would choose which liquors will be served. You might decide to serve wine only. You might decide to have a cash bar available to your guests and make the champagne that is poured at their place for the toast the only complimentary alcoholic beverage. It is extremely difficult to limit your guests to a certain number of drinks, especially since some people will wish to drink far more than others, so liquor may become the one expense you will not be able to predict. As with all aspects of your reception, choose the method that will make the majority of your guests most comfortable. Do remember to have some form of nonalcoholic beverage for children and for those guests who do not drink at all. If possible, check to see if you can purchase all the liquor yourself and have it delivered to the reception site; most establishments with a liquor license will not permit this, since the profit they make on alcoholic beverages is quite high, but it is worth inquiring about if you are watching your budget.

Make arrangements for all the linens and paper products you will need; you will be offered a choice of colors by your caterer or restaurant manager, so you might be able to coordinate the decorations for your reception with the colors chosen for your wedding. Allow at least eight weeks for the printing of any paper products you will want—napkins, matchbooks, souvenir boxes for slices of the groom's cake, place cards. The first name of the bride and groom, or their initials, and the date of the wedding are the typical words and letters printed on these items. Speak to both the caterer and your florist about centerpieces so you can coordinate size, height, color, and style.

If you will assign seating, plan first for the bridal table and the parents' table. The bridal table is the head table and should be placed in the most central location of the arrangement of tables. Everyone should be able to focus on the head table and see the bride and groom, the people they have come to honor. This is often accomplished by using a long rectangular table and setting the places on one side only, so the bridal party may face the other guests. The bridal table should include seating for the members of the wedding party only—spouses or guests of the attendants do not sit here. Flower girls and ring bearers need not sit at the bridal table; they should be seated with their parents. The traditional seating arrangement goes like this: The bride and broom are seated in the center of the place settings, the bride sits to the groom's right. The best man sits next to the bride, the maid of honor sits next to the groom. The ushers and bridesmaids then alternate, male and female, to both ends of (or around) the table. At the parent's table, the parents of both the bride and the groom join the officiator and spouse, the grandparents, and other close relatives whom you feel should be seated in a place of prominence. Customarily, men and women alternate at the parents' table, with the mother of the bride sitting next to the father of the groom. Opposite to them, the father of the bride sits next to the mother of the groom. The officiator should be seated next to one of the bride's parents, his or her spouse next to the other. If the wedding is small, you might decide to have your parents sit at the bridal table. You are not obligated to any form of seating, and if comfort demands that you dispense with tradition, by all means do so. You know your guests best, so you will be able to seat them in a fashion that will prove enjoyable. If you are having a large group of people, you might decide to have a table with all of the place cards on it, and include a small numeral in the corner under the name. Your guests may each pick up their own place card and go to the table that is designated with the same number, an easier method than reading every place card at every table. This process may be planned in reverse. You may provide the head waiter or waitress with an alphabetical listing of your guests; this person would stand in clear view, perhaps a few steps away from the last person in the receiving line, and would direct people to the table they have been assigned to, also designated by a numeral. Even though you and your groom will be expected to speak with each guest at some point during the reception, since your guests are there to be with you, you cannot attempt to be social directors. Guests at a reception should be capable of introducing themselves to one another, many will already be acquainted, and sometimes the strangest combination of personalities will blend beautifully at such a festive occasion! If your parents or your groom's parents are divorced, and will attend the reception, you can diplomatically seat them at tables that are not anywhere near each other. Two parents' tables rather than one may be laid at opposite ends of the room. Everyone's comfort, especially yours, in this situation should be taken into consideration.

The activities that customarily take place at a reception begin with the receiving line. The purpose of a receiving line is to give every guest the opportunity of greeting the newlyweds and the close friends and relatives who will receive with them, and to extend wishes to the couple for their future happiness. You may include the bride, the groom, both sets of parents, and the bridesmaids. The best man (unless he is the groom's father) and ushers do not receive. The receiving line may be abbreviated to include only you and your groom, your mothers, and the maid of honor; these five people are always included in a receiving line. If you choose the latter, the order for the line is this: mother of the bride, mother of the groom, bride, groom, maid of honor. If you choose the former, the order expands to this: mother of the bride, father of the bride, mother of the groom, father of the groom, bride, groom, maid of honor, bridesmaids in the reverse order in which they walked in the processional (therefore, the bridesmaid who led the processional ends the receiving line). Since the bride's father may have duties as host of the affair, he can forego the line even if the groom's father participates in it. Customarily, the bride stands to the groom's right, unless he is in uniform, and no matter who stands where, the bride is usually greeted before the groom. All guests should go through the receiving line, introducing themselves to the mother of the bride and stating their relationship to the bride or groom if they have not met the mother of the bride previously. The people in the receiving line should introduce the guest to the person next in line. Bridesmaids are introduced by their full name, not by a title such as Miss or Mrs. (Carol Stoneman, not Ms. Stoneman). Although the line should not disband until all guests have been received, this implies that all guests will go through the line immediately following their prompt arrival at the reception. Each person in the line should remove any gloves and shake hands with each guest; feel free to kiss or embrace someone close to you and your groom. If a guest is shy, members of the receiving line should introduce themselves and keep the line moving.

Because the bride's mother is usually the hostess of the reception, she is first in the receiving line. If the bride's mother is deceased, the bride's father may stand first in line. If your parents are divorced, the receiving line takes shape according to who is sponsoring the wedding and reception. The host and hostess should be first in line, be they natural or stepparents. If either of the bride's natural parents are attending the wedding as guests, they would not usually receive. If the groom's parents are divorced, usually only his mother joins the receiving line. However, choose feelings over etiquette—if the relationship between divorced parents (and any stepparents) is a good one, they may all agree to participate in the receiving line if you and your groom wish them to do so.

If there is to be no reception, a receiving line may form at the location of the ceremony. A receiving line is not necessary at a reception of fewer than fifty guests. And at a very, very large wedding there is often a person appointed to ask the name of each guest and announce it to the host and hostess and, in extremely formal situations, to the entire group that has gathered in attendance. Obviously, there are many ways of assembling your receiving line; keep its purpose in mind when you decide what will be most effective for your wedding. The purpose, plain and simple, is for you and your groom to meet and greet all of the guests, and to introduce your parents —as well as close friends who have attended you at your wedding ceremony—to people whose acquaintance you wish them to share.

If you wish pictures taken of the receiving line, alert your photographer, for the line will disband as soon as all guests have been greeted so the festivities may officially begin with the seating of the wedding party at the bridal table. Any portrait shots to be taken of the wedding party should be scheduled immediately after the guests have been received, so they will not have to wait to greet you. Making drinks available from the start is a nice way to keep your guests happy during the time it takes to receive and to pose for portrait shots. If a guest book is important to you (it is certainly optional), make arrangements for it to be placed on a table next to the entrance of the reception, or ask a friend to stand at the end of the receiving line to have your guests sign. You might also have that friend take the book to each table during the reception to make sure no one's signature is missing.

Once the guests all take their places, if you have a master of ceremonies, he will alert everyone that the wedding party is about to enter the reception area. You and your party, and your parents if you choose, would then enter as you are introduced by this person. Your parents and your groom's parents would enter first, then your bridesmaids and ushers—in couples, and usually in the order that they marched in the recessional. Your best man and maid of honor would follow them, and finally, a huge fanfare would be sounded to announce the newly married couple. This type of formal announcement is completely up to you; you might choose to simply take your places at the head table without any special drum rolls or salutations. Next, the best man may make the traditional first toast to the bride and groom. This usually involves champagne, and everyone except the bride and groom rise for this. There is a French custom in which the couple drinks from a large marriage cup or bowl and then carries it to each table and serves their guests a sip to symbolize the sharing of their happiness. After the best man makes this toast, he may read aloud any telegrams sent to the couple, usually received from people who were unable to be present.

If you will have dancing at your reception, you will need a specially designated area that is not carpeted. Even though your orchestra or band should play background music from the moment the reception begins and through-out the time it takes for your guests to go through the receiving line, it is customary that no one dance until the bride and groom share their first dance together as husband and wife. They do so after the toast is completed, and the traditional sequence of dancing begins. Here is that traditional order: the bride and groom; the bride and her father, the groom and the mother of the bride; the groom's father and the bride, the groom and his mother. Each set of parents then dance together, the bride dances with the best man, the groom with the maid of honor. Now everyone in the wedding party may join in (the bride should dance with every usher and the groom with every bridesmaid before the dancing ends), followed by all other guests who wish to dance. If you have a favorite song, you should let the orchestra leader know so it can be played for your first dance; the band should also be alerted about any special requests or dedications you may have throughout the party.

The next traditional activity is the cake cutting. This takes place just before dessert if you have had a meal, or approximately one hour after the receiving line disbands if a meal is not being served. The ceremonial cake cutting should be announced so your guests may either circle around the cake table or focus their attention toward you and your groom at this moment. Together, standing to your groom's right and with his hand over yours, you will cut the first slice of cake, (from the bottom layer if the cake is tiered). It is a fun custom to feed each other this first slice, and it will be very tempting to somehow "miss"; this makes a picture that has been included in countless wedding albums. It is a nice gesture to serve your respective parents next; all of the other cutting and serving should be done by your waiters and waitresses. The cake can be a beautiful addition to the decorations of the reception, so make arrangements to have a special table set up for it where it can be admired but not bumped or knocked over.

A short time before you and your groom are ready to go change for your departure, you may want to uphold the traditional tossing of the bridal bouquet and wedding garter. If you have a going-away corsage in the center of your bouquet, hand it to your maid of honor, and have your announcer call everyone together for the throwing of the bouquet. Traditionally, all of the single women will form a group; whoever catches the bouquet is said to be the next to marry. If you wish to be impartial, turn your back and throw it over your shoulder. If you have someone particular in mind to receive it, look at the group and take aim. If you do not wish to uphold this tradition at all, you might like to gather all of the small children together and toss it to them, or present the bouquet to someone special —a grandmother, perhaps. When a prayer book is carried, the ribbons and streamers used to decorate it may be thrown. If you and your groom decide to throw the garter, part one of the ceremony is this: A chair is moved to the center of the dance floor and you sit so your groom may remove the garter from your leg. Then all of the single men gather and the groom throws the garter to them. The tradition is the same: The man who catches it is destined to marry next. While you and your groom go to change, after you have taken a few private moments with your parents to express your personal thanks, your best man will have an opportunity to decorate your getaway car and pull it up to the door for your departure. He might also distribute the rice or confetti that is traditionally showered upon the newlyweds, although birdseed is far more ecological. These last two traditions can also take place after the ceremony, before the ride to the reception.

The members of the wedding party usually are the first arrivals at the reception, and the bride and groom are the first to leave the festivities. Your guests will follow your cue of departure, so take budget into account, because you can control the length of your reception. Room rental and musicians' fees are most likely hourly, so more time and drink than you planned for could increase your expenses substantially. If you have a long journey to make, or if any of your guests have traveled great distances, consider this as well. Your guests may not feel comfortable leaving before you do. If you will be going on a honeymoon immediately, make arrangements for friends to escort or entertain out-of-town guests, particularly if this means either or both sets of parents.

Plan your reception with your entire day's activities in mind. You might wish to schedule an hour or two between the conclusion of your ceremony and the beginning of your reception to allow for picture taking or just some good old-fashioned rest and relaxation. There is no law that says your reception must immediately follow your ceremony; if you would prefer a late evening party after a morning ceremony, just be sure to make the necessary plans. If your wedding and reception will be an all-day affair, perhaps involving travel to a very special site for the festivities, consider all the factors that will be involved in making this feasible for you and your guests.

You are obligated to no particular activities at your reception, or you may choose to have every traditional procedure take place, You are entitled to do what you wish, what your budget allows, and what is tasteful—and thereby practical—for the time of day, the season of the year, the number of guests, and the celebration of your wedding. How would you like your guests to react *after* your reception? If the one comment you would like to hear is "Everyone had a great time," advance planning and concern for your guests will do the trick.

# 19

# SECOND MARRIAGES

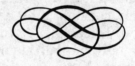

*Stella: He'll be my fourth husband.*

*Seymour: She'll be my fifth wife.*

*Both: And we'll each turn eighty next month.*

Whether you are being married for the second, third, or fourth time, your wedding day is still a "first," the beginning of a new partnership, the sharing of joy that this commitment represents. It is unfortunate that our society designates a marriage as second only if the woman is remarrying. We have grown accustomed to responding differently to people who are marrying again, when the truth is that they are usually marrying each other for the first time! However, as with any festivity or ceremony, early and thorough planning are essential. There are some situations that will be handled differently if you are marrying for the second time, but for the most part, the responsibilities of the bride and groom and their attendants are quite similar to a first-time wedding. The following information will describe details that should be tended to during the planning of your second wedding and will hopefully dispel some of the myths attached to remarriage.

The traditional second wedding has included a very small and informal ceremony with a guest list of no more than fifty persons. There was no processional, the bride was not given away by her father, and there was only one attendant. At the reception, her father did not share a first dance with his daughter, she did not throw her bouquet (if she even carried one), and her wedding cake was pastel, not white. The reception may have been very lavish, with the bride changing from the sedate, street-length suit she wore for the ceremony into a long, elegant gown. Today, throw tradition to the wind and do exactly what will make you, your groom, your families and guests happy.

Your engagement is usually not announced when you are planning to marry for a second time, although you may feel perfectly free to wear an engagement ring. Do plan to announce your marriage. The kind of wedding that will take place is decided by the bride and groom. They may choose a very formal, semiformal, or informal wedding. Many second weddings do include a private nuptial ceremony for the immediate family, which is followed by a large reception or party. You might plan to pay for your own second wedding. If your parents offer to do so, you may indeed graciously accept; however, they probably paid for your first wedding, and you will want to take this into account when planning your second. Often, the bride and groom share the expenses of a second wedding. Couples who do this issue their invitations themselves, although parents of the bride may wish to do so if they are assuming the financial obligations. Invitations for a second marriage are handled in much the same manner as those for a first. Though some etiquette sources say that formal invitations are usually not sent for second marriages, this is only due to the fact that many second weddings include fewer than fifty guests, so personal, handwritten invitations are sent. If you wish to invite more than fifty guests, invitations should be printed, and you may do so formally or informally. The wording and style for a formal invitation is the same as for a first wedding, with the exception of the bride's name. She may use her first, maiden, and married name. However, it is perfectly acceptable for the bride to use her first name together with either her married or maiden name, whichever she is currently using. Those friends and family members whom she will invite to her wedding would never address her as, for example, Mrs. Jones Pressman, and there is no reason to word invitations in that manner. If the ceremony will be private, invitations to the reception may be sent in the traditional manner, issued by the bride and groom or by parents. An invitation to a second wedding hosted by the bride and groom may read:

*The honour of your presence*
*is requested at the marriage of*
*Jane Simmons Thompson*
*to*
*Robert John Maxwell*
*Saturday, the Seventh of February*
*at one o'clock*
*St. Charle's Church*
*Woodstock, Vermont*

An invitation to a reception following a second wedding and hosted by the bride and groom may read:

> *Jane Simmons Thompson*
> *and*
> *Robert John Maxwell*
> *request the pleasure of your company*
> *at their wedding reception*
> *on Saturday, the Seventh of February*
> *at six o'clock*
> *The Inn on the Brook*
> *Woodstock, Vermont*

If the bride's parents are hosting the wedding, the invitation may read:

> *Mr. and Mrs. Albert Simmons*
> *request the honour of your presence*
> *at the marriage of their daughter*
> *Jane Simmons Thompson*
> *to*
> *Robert John Maxwell*

If the bride's parents are issuing an invitation to the reception only, it may read:

> *Mr. and Mrs. Albert Simmons*
> *request the pleasure of your company*
> *at the wedding reception of their daughter*
> *Jane Simmons Thompson*
> *and*
> *Robert John Maxwell*

Legally, only two attendants (one for the bride, one for the groom) are required for any wedding. These persons sign the marriage certificate, acting as the official witnesses for the event. As you plan your second wedding, you may have as many attendants as you wish, but do consider the feelings of those friends or relations who served as attendants at your first wedding. Make sure there will be no misunderstanding if you do not ask them to be a member of your second wedding party. Once you have chosen your attendants, questions may arise regarding showers. Showers are not usually given for a second-time bride, but parties most certainly are. They can be lovely, enjoyable occasions that range from an informal, at-home brunch to more formal evening affairs.

The bride's wedding attire is dependent only on personal taste and the formality of the wedding she and her groom have chosen. The old myth that only a first-time bride may wear white has been replaced with the understanding that white symbolizes the wedding itself rather than the purity of the bride. If a woman decides on a very formal second wedding, she can feel free to wear a traditional gown, although she may decide not to wear a long veil. Some second brides choose not to carry a bouquet or flowers. All of these decisions are strictly personal ones. The groom's attire is governed only by the formality of his bride's dress.

There exist certain distinguishing characteristics that make a wedding ceremony a legal and binding rite. These characteristics must not be ignored because the wedding is a second one for either party. However, many of the nonessential elements may be eliminated—the giving away of the bride, the processional, the recessional. These are items of choice that may be altered or dropped. But the essence of the actual ceremony, the taking of vows and pronouncement of commitment, must be included and should be in grand evidence, as it is the very act you have requested your friends and loved ones to witness.

One of the most distinctive features of a second wedding is the participation of children of the bride or groom in the event. As you embark on your new relationship with your stepchildren, or as your husband-to-be gets to know your children, remember that this is a major change in their lives as well as yours. Take the necessary time to become their friend, their new relative, whatever role you will assume in this family setting. And it will take time. There is no need to compete with the parent who is no longer present—be yourself, be natural, be warm, do not be domineering. If you do not choose to have your children participate in the actual wedding ceremony, perhaps they could perform one of the many necessary duties at the reception. Whether your children are included in the bridal party or not, you might give them a special token, a small gift to demonstrate your desire for them to share in your special day. It is wise to watch words spoken in jest or verbal generalizations that might touch a sensitive chord in a child's emotions, no matter what the age of the offspring may be. We are all our parents' children, and memories are precious. If the words "You are more beautiful than any bride I've ever seen" might be misinterpreted by the groom's young daughter, who is still very close to her natural mother, they are better whispered in private.

As far as your former in-laws and ex-husband go, the situation must be judged strictly on personal ties and feelings. If you are totally estranged from your ex, if there exist no financial obligations, or if you have no children, whether or not you contact him is completely up to you. If you still remain on good terms with your ex-spouse's family and you feel that they would wish to be part of your second wedding day, by all means include them. However, examine this situation openly, discuss it with your husband-to-be, and make your decision together. If there is any doubt as to whether someone might feel uncomfortable, consider the fact that all might run more smoothly if the person were *not* invited. Sometimes this is the best alternative.

As gifts start to arrive for your remarriage, it is often very wise for the bride and groom to each send a thank-you note for the same gift. This is particularly important for children of either spouse and relatives of former spouses. It is a thoughtful gesture that only takes a few more moments of your time, one extra stamp, and an additional note sheet. It can avoid that awkward situation where the bride is a stranger or recent acquaintance and is communicating with a person who has known the groom for years and years. By writing separate notes to children, they will feel the genuine appreciation of their parent and of the person who wants to become an important part of the newly established family structure. Guests who attended your first wedding are under no obligation to send gifts when you are marrying for a second time.

There is absolutely no reason that a second wedding cannot be a happy and glorious event, and the fact that 30 percent of today's weddings are remarriages proves that these are indeed joyful occasions!

## 20
# THANK YOU!—
# GIFT GIVING
# AND RECEIVING

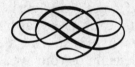

*Thelma: What can I say? I think it's a vase.*

*Theodore: Shhh, here comes Aunt Tallulah now.*

*Both: (smiling nervously) Thank you! It's . . . just what we wanted!*

The moment you announce your intention to wed, gifts will start to arrive for you. Throughout your first year of marriage, you may still receive wedding presents, for it is the accepted rule that a wedding gift may be sent up to one year after the wedding date. And who knows, your great-great-aunt Nellie may decide that she's finally found the perfect gift for you after you celebrate your third anniversary! Whether you receive an enormous amount of goods or just a few tokens of well-wishing, it will be a time when the giving of gifts will be centered upon you and your groom.

There are ways of showing all your friends and relatives what you have received if you choose to display your gifts, and there are also gifts that you will give. However, no matter how you decide to deal with the onslaught of packages, deliveries, boxes, and bows, keep in mind that each gift you receive has been chosen expressly for you and your groom by someone who wishes to add to the joy of your marriage. A thank-you for every gift is absolutely essential, whether the gift is something you've always wanted or something you can't even identify. If you receive your gifts with graciousness and delight, you will reflect the joy that the giver has intended for you, and everyone will share in the special feeling of giving and receiving on the occasion of your wedding.

Gifts are usually given by every guest who accepts your invitation to your reception. Anyone who receives only an invitation to the ceremony, or only an announcement of your marriage, or who must decline your invitation, is not expected to send a gift, although many will probably do so. Technically no one, no matter what priority they may hold on your guest list, is obligated to give a gift. This fact emphasizes even more greatly the need to express your thanks to the donor. You may find that gifts are arriving from people whom you have never met, since gifts are typically sent to the bride's home even if they are from friends or relatives of the groom.

Set up some form of record-keeping system before the first gift arrives. You may decide to use the same type of file card system that you used for your guest list, or you may even use the same cards to keep your records more concise. As you open each gift, you should immediately list it on the card with the donor's name and a brief description of the gift, the date of its arrival, the name of the store where it was purchased in case you wish to make an exchange at a later date, and the date you mail your thank-you note. If you are opening a number of gifts at once, tape the card to the box or to the gift itself, and jot down the date of receipt on the card so you will have the necessary information for entering it into your gift record a bit later. If by any chance you open a gift and do not find a card included, immediately check the return address carefully or call the store from which it was sent to find the donor's name; record it at once.

If you open a gift and it is damaged in any way, contact the store and ask for a replacement. If the gift must be returned, request that the store not mention the damage to the donor. If the gift did not arrive from a specific store or if there was no indication of postal insurance, send a thank-you note with no mention of damage, otherwise the person may feel obliged to send another gift.

If you receive an exact duplicate (and be prepared, for you may receive a triplicate or quadruplicate!) or any gift which is exchangeable that you would like to change with no one the wiser, feel free to do so. However, do not ask where a gift was purchased, and when writing your thank-you note, never mention the exchange or the duplication. If you wait until after your wedding to do any exchanging or returning that you feel is necessary, you may save yourself repetitious trips to certain stores or locales, and you will certainly save yourself the time involved in this kind of shopping. In a practical vein, you might also find that you can combine the dollar amount of more than one gift you are returning to the same store and purchase another larger item that you prefer. If the gift is extremely personal, resign yourself to living with it or storing it, for your friend's feelings are worth far more than an item you would gain in returning the gift for another.

The only time wedding gifts are returned to the donor is if the wedding is canceled. Even if an annulment takes place or the couple divorces immediately, gifts are not returned, and brief thank-you notes are sent without explanation of the situation. In this case, anyone who has not yet sent a gift may be notified with a tactful phone call or note rather than any long discourse on the problems that have arisen. It might be phrased that plans have become indefinite regarding where the couple will be living, or a similar sort of statement may be made.

A thank-you note should be handwritten for each gift you receive, even if the donor is someone that you see every day, a close friend or relative, or someone that you have thanked by telephone or in person. The only people who need not receive a handwritten note are you, your groom, and both sets of parents; however, you might decide to send a beautiful letter or flowers to your parents in thanks. If you can, send the thank-you note as soon as you receive the gift. Since this will be close to impossible, especially as you approach your wedding day, just make sure that your thank-you notes are written within one month of your return from your honeymoon if you will depart for a trip immediately following your wedding day. The outside limit for thank-you writing is three months from the wedding; this should only happen if your wedding is extremely large or if you are planning an extended journey following your wedding. If either of these situations are the case, you might consider sending an engraved or printed card of acknowledgment to the donor so that he or she will know that the gift has been received. These cards should be sent immediately upon receipt of the gift, and they do not replace the writing by hand of a personal note of thanks at the later date.

Thank-you notes may be very brief, but should be

quite specific about the gift received. If a check is sent, it is nice to suggest what you and your groom will purchase with the money. Thank-you notes are usually written on plain notepaper or note cards (stationers call these cards *informals*); they may be written on stationery with your married monogram after the wedding has taken place. Only use stationery with the monogram of your maiden name before the actual ceremony, and remember that this may be confusing to people receiving the note if you sign it with a name other than your maiden name, or if you use both your name and your groom's name together. There are also cards that may be purchased that leave two blanks for you to fill in, one for the gift and one for your name, but they are very impersonal. It will only take a few moments longer to write a sentence or two of thanks in your hand, and that is far more meaningful to your gift givers.

Feel free to address thank-you notes to relatives you do not know well in the manner that your groom does, and he should do the same for your relatives. If you call Aunt Nellie "Auntie Nellie," and he is writing that particular note, he may refer to her as you do; she is now his relative, too. If you have received a gift from a couple, address both people (in the past, it used to be considered proper to write only to the woman). If you receive a gift from a group, co-workers, or fellow members of an organization, you may write one note to them collectively, listing each of their names (Dear blank, blank, blank, blank, and blank), or addressing them in an affectionate term such as "My dear friends."

There was a time when gifts were customarily addressed to the bride, so it was felt that she should correctly write all the thank-you notes herself. Today there is no reason your groom can't assist in the thank-you writing. Whoever is writing a particular note mentions the other spouse and signs the note. If you agree to compose your letter in the first person plural, "we," do sign your last name or names if you do not know the giver well. The person's hand that wrote the note may sign both names.

You and your groom do have a method of expressing your desire for any specific gifts by registering those preferences at the department or specialty stores of your choice. This free service is called bridal registry, and almost all major stores offer it to couples who are planning to marry. You and your groom should choose items you will live with for a long time together—china, silver, crystal, and linens. All of these may be registered, but don't forget to list other items you will need. Do so in a wide price range, so all of your guests will feel comfortable purchasing something they know you have chosen. Most stores will list everything they carry in their inventory in every department throughout the store. If one of your families is from a city that is far away, register the patterns you have chosen and the items you have selected in branches of department stores or local shops in that city so friends there may take advantage of this method of gift giving. A store that offers registry service will keep continuous, accurate records of what has been purchased for you; this will help solve the problem of duplication and will make returning and exchanging much easier. You might also decide that you would prefer to have china now and crystal later; at your request, the store will designate your crystal-pattern listing as "filled" and will thereby encourage the purchase of the dinnerware. Keep in touch with the salesperson at the store as you receive gifts to make sure that your records agree with theirs. Inform the store of where you wish to have gifts sent; if you and your groom are moving to a new address, you may want gifts sent there rather than to your mother's home, which is the customary place that presents are sent. You can plan to have presents stored at the shop and shipped at one time; make arrangements with the store to notify you as soon as a gift is purchased so you can send the thank-you note.

If you are going to register dinnerware, flatware, and glassware, make sure that you coordinate the patterns of all three in the style that you and your groom prefer. You will be amazed at the variety available to you, so take the time to shop around, pick and choose. You are also entitled to mix plain and fancy if you so desire. The term *glassware* refers to everything from cut crystal for elegant dinner parties to large balloon wineglasses that can be used every day for orange juice. Pick up the glasses, hold them up to the light, and check for smoothness and balance; tap crystal to listen for the resonant ring that quality glass will produce. Your salesperson should show you all the pieces that belong to a place setting; handle each plate and glass to make sure they will be comfortable for you.

*Flatware* refers to all the utensils used for eating, be they silver or stainless steel. The latter has become very popular today, and the heavier the stainless steel is, the better the quality. The metal to decide upon is your number one question, then proceed to choosing the pattern in that metal that appeals to you. Daily use of silver actually helps to create a patina that will add to its attractiveness over the years. The monogrammed gift is diminishing in popularity because of the more casual life-style most couples are choosing and because a monogrammed gift is never returnable or even exchangeable. It is wiser to have any monogramming you may choose for your silver ordered after the gift is given so you and your groom can make your own decisions about lettering and style.

Linens are now available in many easy-to-care-for fabrics, as well as the traditional cotton, percale, silk, satin, and muslin. Cotton and cotton percale are extremely durable, but the care required for them must also be considered. Decide which linen items you would like; if you want tablecloths and napkins, you will need at least as many napkins as you plan to have place settings; colors and styles of towels, bedsheets, and the like will influence the entire look of a room.

*China* is a term that is applied to all types of dinnerware from fine china made of bone or porcelain to everyday dishes of stoneware or earthenware.

The other form of unofficial registry is the word-of-mouth system by which you let your mother, your groom's mother, and very close friends know the gifts you would really like to receive. Do not be shy about this, for if people have no guidelines whatsoever, you may spend countless hours exchanging, returning, and storing. If you need a new vacuum and already have a beautiful set of crystal goblets, speak up. The combination of a store registry and your own openness to the people closest to you should provide friends with the information they need to purchase the gift you'd like.

Some couples decide to display their gifts for everyone to see. Gift displays are often set up a week or two before the wedding and are left intact for a week or two after the event. This is a custom that is in no way obligatory, but if you decide to display there are a few important procedures to keep in mind. You should use a space in your home that can be designated for this purpose solely, probably one that is not used continuously. You might cover a table with a floor-length white cloth; not only will this show off the gifts well, but you can store all the boxes underneath the table. You might add some flowers and greens for a decorative effect. Arrange the presents so no duplicates are next to each other and so gifts of the same category are side by side. Save space by only displaying one place setting of your china, glassware, and flatware. You must decide if you will display cards to indicate the donors as well. There are pros and cons to this. If you do so, no one will ask who the donor was; if you don't display cards, no one will compare size, quantity, or price. Checks and gift certificates may be displayed under glass, but they should be placed so the name, not the amount, is visible. This can be achieved easily by overlapping the checks like playing cards. You might opt for a small card that reads "check from Uncle John and Aunt Nellie," and get the money safely and directly to the bank upon receipt rather than displaying it at all. If you do display, include every single gift and do any returning or exchanging after the wedding. Make sure that you investigate the short-term insurance policy called a floater, which is available for gift displays. At very large, well-publicized weddings, people have been known to hire security guards for the times they will be away from the display, including the rehearsal, wedding, and reception.

If any of your guests bring gifts to the reception, it is wise to appoint a friend or relative who is not a member of the wedding party to take charge of the gifts, making sure they are kept in a safe place during the festivities and transported to your home afterward. Gifts are not opened at the reception, so make an alternate plan for recording their arrival if you will be departing for your wedding trip directly from your reception. Your mother or your maid of honor might take charge of this task if you will be away for a long period of time. If not, you can write your thank-you as soon as you return. Any checks that are given before the wedding are usually made out to the bride in her maiden name, and checks given after the wedding are made out to the married couple. You may receive numerous envelopes containing checks or cash throughout the reception; make sure that you have a place to guarantee their safekeeping, be it a traditional money bag or your groom's inside jacket pocket.

Although you and your groom will receive much more than you give, there are specific persons whom you will want to thank with a small gift or memento of your wedding. A bride usually gives all her attendants the same gift, with the exception of the maid of honor, who should receive a token that is a bit more extravagant, since she will devote the most time and service to the bride. The groom will give his ushers identical gifts, as well as the accessories for their wedding attire. His best man should get something a little more special than the ushers for the same reason that the maid of honor does: He will give a greater amount of time and effort than the other grooms-men. You and your groom may decide to give both sets of parents a small remembrance of the wedding to express your thanks; this is an optional item on your gift-giving list, but is certainly a nice gesture of appreciation. If you and your groom decide to have the gifts you choose for your attendants engraved, allow at least two to four weeks for this. Custom has dictated that the groom's parents usually give a generous gift to the couple, sometimes the entire honeymoon trip, and the parents of the bride give an impressive gift for the newlyweds' home. Those decisions are completely up to your parents, but they would probably be glad to know of your wants and needs, so do not hesitate to discuss them with these people, who are probably the very closest to you. Your attendants give gifts, and bridesmaids and ushers might decide to do so jointly or as two separate groups. Often the bridesmaids will choose a gift specifically for the bride and the ushers will do the same for the groom because of their close friendship to each person. If a group gift is given, all persons involved should receive a separate thank-you note since the group as a whole does not work or congregate at one particular address. They are a group at your request. Finally, you and your groom will probably wish to uphold the tradition of exchanging gifts; you can surprise each other, or hint, or just come right out and say what you'd like. The only item that is exchanged infrequently between couples is clothing, but this choice is yours and yours alone.

As you and your groom make the selection of the gifts you will give, remember all the people who have volunteered any form of service: musicians, a soloist, friends who will act as chauffeurs, relatives who will take charge of special tasks at the reception, your flower girl and ring bearer. Anyone who is not paid for services rendered should probably receive a gift and definitely receive a thank-you note from both of you.

Remember the old adage, "It's the thought that counts." Each of your donors has put thought and consideration into whatever they have chosen to give to you and your groom. It might not be the present of your dreams, but it still deserves an expression of thanks. Anyone who gives a gift on the occasion of a marriage is wishing you a lifetime of happiness rather than just recognizing the celebration of an event. The gift is their way of attempting to make some form of contribution to that happiness, but the wish alone is something to be grateful for.

## 21
# UNUSUAL CIRCUMSTANCES

*Ursula: Did you know they're going to have a triple wedding on top of a mountain at dawn?*

*Ulysses: I thought it was three consecutive weddings in a cave at midnight.*

*Both: Set the alarm, we don't want to be late.*

Although no wedding is typical or normal to its participants, some conditions are unusual. Perhaps unique is a better word—it would still place this chapter under *U*! Whatever circumstances surround your marrying, there are ways and means of dealing with them. No problem is too great to solve, no novel idea too impossible to produce, as long as you remain within the bounds of good taste. This chapter will list a few examples of some instances that occur more infrequently, but are nonetheless realistic and require special attention if the situation arises for you.

## Double Wedding

If two sisters or two friends decide to combine their separate wedding ceremonies into one, this is called a double wedding. There are a variety of ways to handle this situation. Attendants may be shared or each bride and groom may have their own. The brides and grooms may serve as the honor attendants for each other; this keeps the wedding party a bit smaller. The two parties need not dress identically, although there must be a coordination of colors in fabrics and flowers. The older sister may be escorted by her father and walks down the aisle first with her attendants, followed by her younger sister, who would be escorted by an uncle, brother, or close friend of the family, and her attendants. The ushers (both sets) would walk down the aisle together before either bride. If the brides share attendants, they could have their father walk between them as they march down the aisle. The older bride and her attendants stand to the left for the ceremony. If the brides are not sisters, but friends, their mothers may share the first pew, with the senior mother nearer the aisle. The fathers of the brides join them there after escorting their daughters down the aisle. Both brides' families and both grooms' families may share the left and right sides of the church or hall respectively. In the recessional, the older bride is followed by the younger.

The receiving lines for a double wedding of two friends who share no attendants form in the traditional fashion and may be next to each other or on opposite sides of the entry to the reception. If the brides are sisters, if attendants are shared, or if one receiving line rather than two is preferred, that line may be formed in this order: older bride's mother and her groom's mother, younger bride's mother (if brides are friends, not sisters), mother of groom of younger bride, older bride, her husband, her maid of honor, younger bride, her husband, her maid of honor.

Invitations may be worded in the traditional manner, with the addition of the phrase "at the marriage of their daughters." The older bride's name and the name of her fiancé are stated first. If the brides are not sisters, but friends, their surnames are included on the invitation.

*Mr. and Mrs. John Paul Smith*
*request the honour of your presence*
*at the marriage of their daughters*
*Susan Elizabeth*
*to Mr. James Peter Black*
*and*
*Elizabeth Susan*
*to*
*Mr. Peter James White*


*Mr. and Mrs. Steven Miller*
*and*
*Mr. and Mrs. Robert Baker*
*request the honour of your presence*
*at the marriage of their daughters*
*Mary Martha Miller*
*to*
*Mr. Ralph Edward Cook*
*and*
*Blair Barbara Baker*
*to*
*Mr. Henry Alexander Farmer*

The easy rule for double weddings seems to be that just as in order of birth, the older leads the way.


## Military Weddings

Military weddings are formal by virtue of the fact that full-dress uniforms are worn by the men, a long dress is worn by the bride, and all military protocol is carried out. Only commissioned officers may plan a military wedding; reserve officers may not do so unless they are on active duty. Also, the traditional arch of sabres, or swords, may only be formed by commissioned officers, and at least four military ushers are needed to do so. The arch is formed inside the church (if the church permits) at the command of the head usher, when the newly married couple turns to face the congregation. The bride and groom walk under the arch at the conclusion of the ceremony; they traditionally use the sword to cut the cake. The uniformed men wear all their military decorations, but do not wear boutonnieres. Any usher who is not a member of the military wears attire that is appropriate to the formality of the occasion.

An invitation or announcement for a military wedding includes rank. This title is printed before the groom's name if it is captain or above in the Army or Air Force, commander or above in the Navy, or major or above in the Marine Corps. Under his name the branch of service may be printed, if desired. If rank is any lower, it is printed with the branch of service under the groom's full name, and *Mr.* is omitted. If the groom is an enlisted man or has not been commissioned, his branch of service is printed under his name and *Mr.* is omitted. A bride who is in military service would include her rank and branch of service under her name.

*Captain Peter Paul Smith*
*United States Army*

*Peter Paul Smith*
*Lieutenant, United States Army*

*Peter Paul Smith*
*United States Army*

*at the marriage of their daughter*
*Mary*
*Lieutenant, Women's Army Corps*

## Fathers and Grooms Who Are Clergymen

Here are two situations that don't happen very often, but details are easily arranged if they do. If your father is a clergyman and you wish him to act as officiator for your wedding ceremony, he may certainly do so. Obviously, he would not uphold the tradition of giving the bride away, but your mother may step forward to do this when the question is asked. The bride may be escorted down the aisle by a brother, her godfather, an uncle, or a close friend.

If your groom is a clergyman, you must decide if you wish to be married in your church or his. If you choose the latter, your groom's immediate superior should officiate, and your groom would not wear any of the clerical vestments. He may, however, wear his clerical collar.

## A Bride Without Parents

If a bride is an orphan, or if her parents are unable to participate in the wedding due to extenuating circumstances, the groom's parents may decide to host the entire event. This is certainly acceptable, and the invitations would include the words "their son" to avoid confusion, although this is not essential.

## *An Unusual Second Marriage*

If you and your husband have been divorced and decide to remarry, you need not send out a formal announcement that uses the copy of a normal wedding announcement. Formal announcements are not correct in this situation; use your own fine discretion in writing simple copy for a note that will be sent to those acquaintances and business associates that you and your husband feel must be informed of your new status.

## *Divorced Parents*

There are very tactful ways to deal with the situation of four parents rather than two. Most importantly, everyone's feelings must be considered, but the bride and groom should not have to sacrifice any of the plans they have made for their wedding day. Hopefully, all parents will make every effort to contribute to their children's happiness by complying with the wishes of the bride and groom. A great amount of sensitivity and understanding may be called into play; if a recently divorced parent has begun dating someone new, perhaps this new person should not attend the wedding. If the bride's parents are divorced but on amicable terms, they may still act as official host and hostess, and the father will pay for all—or at least half—of the expenses. If the bride's parents have been divorced for a long period of time, the mother of the bride may sponsor the wedding. If both of the bride's parents have remarried, both the natural and stepparents may wish to sponsor the wedding together, in which case all four could even stand in the receiving line. Use good judgment and honest discussion in these cases, because it is also relatively simple to have two parents' tables that are not next to each other at the reception and to have your divorced parents stand at opposite ends of the receiving line. At the actual wedding ceremony, divorced parents need not sit together. The bride's or groom's mother sits in the first pew, with her husband if she has remarried (or with a very close relative if she has not remarried and would feel more comfortable being seated with another person), and the bride's or groom's father sits in the second or third pew, with his current wife (or a close relative if he has not remarried and so chooses). Tradition says the third pew, although the choice is yours. You and your husband-to-be know your respective parents well enough to handle the divorced-parents situation with relative ease (no pun intended), but do be firm in achieving your own wishes for the smooth running of your wedding day.

### A Broken Engagement or Cancelled Wedding

The only thing that may be worse than a broken engagement is a miserable marriage. Better to end a relationship that will not work before it begins; no one needs to be given a lengthy explanation. If formal wedding invitations have been sent, formal cancellation announcements should be sent if time permits. If not, let the information be known as quickly as possible via telephone or telegram. Notify all of your suppliers (caterers, photographer, baker, florist), your officiator, and all invited guests. The announcement may simply be worded thus: "Mr. and Mrs. John Smith announce that the marriage of their daughter, Amy, to Mr. Robert Jones will not take place." If the engagement has been announced in newspapers and is broken prior to wedding invitations being sent, you may place a brief announcement in the same newspapers that reads: "Mr. and Mrs. John Smith announce that the engagement of their daughter, Amy, and Mr. Robert Jones has been ended by mutual consent." If informal wedding invitations have been mailed, send a brief note, which need only state that the wedding will not take place.

Any wedding gifts that have been received in these situations should be returned. The only exception to this rule is a gift that includes a monogram; you can only express thanks and remember that this person does not have to give an expensive gift if either you or your ex-fiancé do marry at a later date. You may choose to send gifts back with a very short note; you will thereby avoid a situation where a friend will force you to keep the gift for yourself.

Unpleasant as all of this may sound, you can handle a broken engagement or a cancelled wedding with great dignity, and you need not feel embarrassed in any way. Any private matters are yours and yours alone.

### Postponement of the Wedding

A death or a serious illness in the family of either the bride or the groom may necessitate the postponement of the wedding date. Alert all of your suppliers immediately. You may decide that you wish to hold your wedding on the scheduled day and at the appointed hour, but that you will not hold the reception. Either of these situations may be handled with printed announcements if time permits. If not, a note may be handwritten. The following format may be used:

*Mr. and Mrs. John Jones*
*regret that they are obliged to recall*
*the invitations to the marriage of their daughter*
*Amy*
*to*
*Mr. Robert Smith*
*owing to the death of Mr. Smith's mother*
*Mrs. Robert Smith, Sr.*

If you decide to be married at the scheduled time and still wish your guests to attend the wedding, but will cancel the reception, you may use the same format above, substituting "the invitations to the marriage reception" and include the date. Then state, "The marriage ceremony will take place as originally planned."

If you decide to be married privately and wish your guests to be aware of this, you may add the following line to the format above: "The ceremony will be held privately in the presence of the immediate family."

If you have chosen an official date on which you will reschedule your wedding, you may state that information.

> *Mr. and Mrs. John Jones*
> *announce that the marriage of their daughter*
> *Amy*
> *to*
> *Mr. Robert Smith*
> *has been postponed from*
> *Saturday, the Seventh of February*
> *until*
> *Saturday, the Fourth of April*
> *at twelve noon*
> *St. Timothy's Church*
> *Ambler, Pennsylvania*

Needless to say, those friends and relations who would have joined you in the happiness of your wedding day will share in your sorrow, and will be most understanding in a matter of such gravity. If anything, you will probably not have to make a great effort to notify guests, except for the fact that clarity and immediacy in these matters do require the written word.

Since many of the situations described above are not blissful ones, remember that any possible wedding circumstance can usually be handled with efficiency and diplomacy. If you and your groom feel that you must be married at dawn overlooking the ocean, just plan to devote the extra effort to make the arrangements and take the additional time to explain these plans to a relative who might not share your feelings on first learning of your choices. But sincerity, courtesy, and taste will help you handle any unusual circumstance that occurs as you plan your wedding.

## 22
# VOWS AND VEILS—
# WEDDING
# TRADITIONS

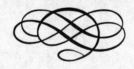

*Vera: Vernon, there's been a tradition in my family for some years now. It's just a little bit corny, but we consider it very important. See, I carry you across the threshold. Wanna know why?*

*Vernon: You what?*

*Both: Good Luck!*

Rites of marriage are as old as humanity, and few others are couched in so many traditions. Chinese marriage laws go back at least four thousand years, and some of the most common traditions upheld today can be traced to ancient

158

civilizations. Marriages have united nations and provoked battles, and many of the most important events in history have taken place at weddings. Traditions are customs and beliefs that are passed from generation to generation without written instruction. They can be beautiful additions to your wedding celebration, and the understanding of their origins will make your wedding even more meaningful. Here described are some of the most standard and commonly practiced customs that have been handed down through the years. They are listed in traditional alphabetical order:

### Bridal Wear

Bridal dresses are traditionally white because of the early Greek belief that white symbolized purity, innocence, and joy. Although this implies naiveté, the white or ivory bridal dress has come to symbolize the wedding itself, rather than the virginal status of the bride. White is also a symbol of celebration; it may be worn for second weddings as well as first. Lace, considered a work of art in Europe, was often used for festive celebrations and important occasions. Even peasant women wore wedding aprons made of lace, but because of the then-prohibitive cost of this beautiful fabric, its use was often limited to nobility. A lace mantilla was given by the groom to his bride in Spain because it was considered such a treasure. She wore this in place of a veil. The wearing of a wedding veil has been handed down from ancient times; it originally expressed modesty and privacy. Many countries held that a bride should be completely hidden from her groom, and the long veil served this purpose. This custom is still practiced today in many foreign countries; the bride is often entirely covered, with only her eyes showing. In India the bride is wrapped in fabrics of vibrant colors and the groom wears white! In early America, when Major

Lawrence Lewis, aide to President Washington, married Nelly Custis, she wore a long veil. She chose lace for her veil because the major had complimented her on her appearance after catching a glimpse of her through the lace curtain of an open window. She probably began this fashion trend in the United States. Traditionally, bridesmaids and ushers dress like the bride and groom to confuse the evil spirits. These spirits could not be sure which woman was the bride and which man the groom because the entire wedding party was attired in the same fashion; therefore, they refrain from any unfortunate curses. The anonymous poem that contains the quote "Something old, something new, something borrowed, something blue, and a lucky sixpence in your shoe" is probably the most famous of all dictates on what to wear on your wedding day. Something old can be an heirloom jewel, a small prayer book, an antique handkerchief originally carried by the bride's mother or grandmother. It could also be a wedding dress that was handed down from the bride's mother. If the bride wears a token that has been given to her by a happily married woman, not only the rule of something old will be followed, but it is said that the good fortune of the giver's happiness will be passed down to the bride. Something new could be the bride's wedding gown or her floral bouquet. Something borrowed could be the heirloom article described above, it could be a personal item lent by a dear friend, or it could be something blue. The Israelites believed that blue signified constancy, or permanency, in relationships. The traditional blue garter fits this category; in ancient times, the garter symbolized the release of the virgin girdle. If you decide not to wear the garter, you may choose to place a small blue bow on your crinoline or have a special small monogram sewn on the inside of your gown. The lucky sixpence is often a shiny silver dime placed inside the bride's shoe, and many families save the coin and pass it on to other relatives.

## Ceremonial Traditions

The giving away of the bride by her father comes from the historical time when women were treated as property, and a price had been paid by the man to whom the father would give the bride. This tradition has changed greatly as time has gone by, and the giving away of the bride has become a sign of approval of the marriage on the part of the parents of the bride. At the conclusion of the ceremony, tradition maintains that the groom must be the first person to kiss the bride. This symbolizes their faith and love and seals the confidences that they share privately. From ancient times, a kiss has signified respect and obedience to mutual beliefs; the kissing of a ruler's ring or the ground upon which he walked was practiced throughout history.

## Flowers

Flowers have been a part of wedding celebrations for centuries. In ancient Roman times the bride would carry herbs under her veil. This custom gave way to the carrying of orange blossoms as a symbol of fertility. There is a Roman myth in which the goddess Juno gives Jupiter a golden apple on their wedding day to bring the guarantee of happiness. Both British poets Spenser and Milton interpreted this golden apple as an orange; hence, orange blossoms have become a traditional wedding flower. By the fourteenth century, in France, all the guests at a wedding rushed for the bride's garter at the end of the ceremony because its possession was considered great luck. It became quickly apparent that people were often getting hurt, so the bride began to remove the garter herself and throw it to the group. The custom of throwing bouquets had its origin here. The bride throws her bouquet to all the unmarried women, and the one who catches it is said to be the next to marry. In the late 1800s, in the U.S., a bride often carried a group of small bouquets numbering the same as her maids. These bouquets were tied together, and a ring was hidden inside one of the small floral arrangements. When the time came for the bride and groom to steal away, the room was darkened, the bride untied the bouquet, then she threw the flowers to her guests. This provided quite a lot of activity as everyone scrambled for the bouquet with the ring to see who would be the next married, and amidst all the confusion, the bride and groom could secretly exit. Some people hold that the long ribbons that decorate the bride's bouquet should be tied with a row of knots along their length; the bride may make a wish for each knot. One of these wishes should be for the happiness of the person who catches her bouquet; the knots should never be untied or the wishes won't come true.

### Honeymoons

The ancient Teutons gave us the first honeymoon and the origin of the word *bridal*. They celebrated the marriages in their country of Germany with great feasting and drinking. A special wine was brewed from honey and yeast, and they drank this wine for thirty days, from one full moon (under which the couple was married) to the next. From this custom the word *honeymoon* was coined, and because the drink was called *brydealo* or *brideale*, the word *bridal* is still used today. There was a time when the bride was captured and hidden away by her groom until her kinspeople stopped their search for her. This "getaway" following marriage is also linked to the origin of today's honeymoon.

## *Jewels*

Historically, rings both had a monetary value and symbolized emotional commitment. Rings date back to a time when brides were bought and sold; they were used as payment to the family for the bride. The very early ones were made of braided grass; later, expensive metal demonstrated the buyer's wealth. An engagement ring was partial payment for the bride and confirmed the groom's well-meaning intentions.

In A.D. 1215, Pope Innocent III declared that not only must weddings take place in churches, but a waiting period must be observed between betrothal and marriage. This led to the separate wedding ring; since an engagement did not necessarily result in a wedding, the ring was permitted to be a broken circle—broken with a gem. From the fifteenth century A.D., diamonds have been the most popular engagement gem because they are the most durable stone found in all geological discovery. The first diamond engagement rings were worn in medieval Italy.

Rings have not only been used as payment. From the time of the ancient Egyptians, an unbroken circular wedding band has symbolized unending love and commitment to a permanent relationship. The ring, which replaced the crowns worn in certain ancient cultures (and still used in certain ethnic wedding ceremonies), signified the eternal circle, which had no beginning and no end. Thus should be the love between husband and wife. The ancients placed the ring on the third finger of the left hand because they believed that the vein in that finger led directly to the heart. Tradition varies on this; Greek women wear their rings on the right hands as do people in certain European countries. The American custom has always been to wear the ring on the left hand. There has been a resurgence of ring wearing in the U.S. Statistics show that 94 percent of today's grooms are wearing wedding bands, which emphasizes the fact that the popularity of traditions rises and wanes often.

### Luck, Good and Bad

The wishing of good luck and the avoidance of bad have been the bases for the development of many wedding traditions. Many of the customs have to do with the wish for fruitful productivity and fertility. The ancient Romans believed that the goddess Vesta, who ruled over the hearth and the threshold, was connected with virgins. It was therefore considered bad luck for a new bride to stumble or trip as she entered her new home. From this belief came the tradition that the groom carries the bride over the threshhold. It was also the ancient Romans who originated the tradition of throwing rice at the newly married couple. They would break thin pieces of wheat bread over the head of the bride because they considered grain and rice to be symbols of fertility. It was their way of wishing the couple many offspring. The guests would quickly chase after the crumbs, because they were believed to be good luck symbols. Old shoes, which are now tied to the back of the honeymoon car, used to be a symbol of authority and possession. The father of the bride would give the groom an old shoe that had been worn by the bride, signifying his transference of authority over her to the husband. Rice, confetti, rose petals, and old shoes have all become signs of good luck today. Ecologically minded people use birdseed instead of confetti, and festive friends decorate cars with colorful streamers rather than old shoes, but the wishes for good fortune remain the same.

There is an old saying that reads "Blest is the bride

on whom the sun doth shine." It comes from a time when certain months of the year were considered far luckier for marriage than others, and since the ancients believed that the sun was the great source of fertilizing power, the months in which the sun shone brightly were felt to be better months for marriage. Just as the sun was a great influence on reproductive capacity, the moon was thought to be the guardian of lovers, so the month of June—when the moon shines more brightly—was felt to be an excellent time to be married. June is still considered one of the most popular wedding months today. Because of this ancient belief in the powers of the sun and the moon, many weddings took place outside, and brides in Eastern countries always faced the east, where the sun rose, as they arose on the morning of their wedding. This tradition is one that is greatly influenced by climate; in the northern, colder countries of Norway and Iceland, it is believed that a wedding that takes place during a blizzard will be advantageous, because the storms of life would then be over for the newlyweds.

There are some superstitions that are better ignored; there was a time when it was believed that a bride should not rehearse her wedding, that it would bring bad luck, and that she should have a substitute walk through the rehearsal for her. It is much wiser to participate in —rather than just watch or not attend—your rehearsal, so you feel totally prepared for your wedding ceremony. There was also a belief that if one congratulated the bride, this would imply that she had trapped her husband; it was felt that the groom, who had pursued and won his wife, should be offered congratulations. Today the word *congratulations* is understood to be an expression of pleasure for the couple's good fortune and happiness and may be offered to both the bride and groom.

In eighteenth-century Scandinavia, a legend unfolded which holds that chimney sweeps were the bearers of good luck. This was because the people found that the incidence of house fires decreased greatly once the chimney sweeps finished their work. If a chimney sweep gives the bride a kiss at her wedding, it is considered the best of luck; in many towns, the sweeps, wearing their uniforms of top hats and tails, still regularly attend wedding ceremonies today. Invite one to yours!

### Parties and Showers

It is held that showers began in Holland. A Dutch father did not approve of the poor miller whom his daughter wished to marry, so her friends "showered" her with gifts so she would have the necessary dowry to gain her father's permission to marry the man of her choice. Today, gifts for a bride's trousseau are often given at wedding showers. This word stems from the French word for bundle, *trusse*. In France, this word was the name for the bundle of clothing and household necessities that the bride brought to her new home. A trousseau also contributed to the dowry of unmarried daughters, who thus became more valuable to possible suitors. There are two more contemporary traditions that characterize showers today. Since many brides have a majority of the household articles they need for their new home (many couples find that they have two of everything already because they have each been living in separate apartments or homes that are fully equipped), the hostess of the shower will specify a certain gift category that she knows the bride would prefer (kitchen, lingerie, new patio). The bride should let her maid of honor or mother know what she would like "just in case" a shower is given. One of the categories that has become more popular in recent years is cash, called a purse shower or a greenback shower. This may sound impersonal, but in many cases it proves to be a far more valuable gift to the bride and groom, one which will give them the opportunity of purchasing a larger item that they would otherwise not have been given. The amounts need not be disclosed publicly, and the party can be just as festive as the bride opens humorous cards or funny packages.

The second custom that has developed with the advent of gift wrapping and ribbon is this: One person is put in charge of collecting all the ribbons and bows from the packages the bride opens. These decorative items are tied together to form a bouquet which the bride may carry at the wedding rehearsal.

The traditional bridesmaids' party includes the serving of a cake into which has been baked a ring or small trinket. Whichever maid is served this piece is said to be the next to marry. There is also an historical reference for the origin of gift giving to the attendants. There was a time when the groom and his attendants went to the home of the bride to claim her; they were not permitted to enter until they gave the maids who protected the bride some form of gift. Today, both the bride and the groom give their attendants gifts of thanks for their assistance and participation in the wedding and all of its planning. The gift has become a symbol of friendship rather than bargaining.

The traditional bachelor party is held in honor of the groom as he shares his last few hours of single status with his ushers, best man, and other good friends. Some people consider this party a last fling, and various and sundry activities may be planned for entertainment. Customarily, the groom proposes a toast to his bride, after which all the drinkers break their glasses as a symbol that the glass may never be used for another less worthy intention.

Today, parties and showers are given for the bride and groom together, and there are numerous variations on the theme of these festive events. Feel free to start your own tradition!

## Wedding Cakes

In medieval England it was the custom for each guest to bring a bun or small cake to the wedding. These sweets were piled one on top of the other, and the bride and groom would kiss over the stack. A French chef who watched this lovely custom decided to spread icing over the small cakes, and thus the first tiered wedding cake was created. To this day, the bride and groom cut the first slice of the wedding cake together to insure their future happiness. Superstition holds that for anyone else to do so might cut into their joy and prosperity. The groom's cake is traditionally a dark, rich fruitcake, said to provide the couple with blessings of fertility. This cake is often kept for the return of the couple to their own home from their honeymoon, or it may be sliced and given to the guests to take home as a souvenir. The first slice of this cake may also be cut by the bride and groom to guard against the possibility of someone cutting into their future bliss. The top tier of a multitiered wedding cake is traditionally kept and frozen by the bride and groom; they save this layer for the celebration of their first anniversary.

Traditions can add the beautiful touches to your wedding that all your guests enjoy. Every country and every religion hold their own customs, some of which date back to the very origin of the nation or sect. The Quakers sign their marriage certificate before the entire congregation. The Amish marry on Tuesdays or Thursdays. The Jewish wedding is held under a *Chuppah,* a canopy that covers the bride, groom, and rabbi, and the bride's mother and father accompany her down the aisle for the ceremony. At a Spanish wedding the flower girl, called the *la portora de anillos,* is dressed exactly like the bride, a miniature version of the marrying woman. Any library or religious official can give you history on a custom you may wish to investigate—or feel free to start your own, if it has a very special meaning to you, your groom, and the people with whom you wish to share your wedding day.

# 23
# WEDDING CAKES

*W*anda: *Vanilla.*

*W*aldo: *Chocolate.*

*B*oth: *Marble.*

There was once a civil wedding ceremony after which the
bride and groom took a knife and together cut into a pile
of three prepackaged cupcakes stacked on a paper plate.
They fed each other their first bite, and the justice of the
peace, his wife, and their other witness all partook of this
feast with a far greater amount of smiles than cake! The
one edible item that seems to define a wedding reception,

large or small, is the wedding cake. So whether you decide on a traditional cake of several tiers or the plate of cupcakes, the cake-cutting ceremony and the sharing of a confection with guests are a delight.

Make plans to meet with the baker and order your cake three months in advance. If you haven't a specific person in mind, you could contact the food editor or style editor of your local newspaper and ask for a recommendation. Feel free to ask the baker if you may not only see samples but taste a sample, especially if you are ordering any kind of cake that is out of the ordinary. Explain the theme of your wedding, the approximate number of guests that will attend the reception, and any specific flavors or color of decoration you might want. Be prepared with a list of any other baked items you may want the baker to provide—small portions of cake for guests to take home, any breadstuffs for an at-home reception, pastries or croissants for a breakfast for out-of-town guests the day after the wedding. Discuss prices and leave your deposit. Make sure that you get, in writing, a detailed receipt describing the size, flavor, and decoration of the cake; filling, if necessary; delivery date, time, and address; and balance to be paid. Ask your baker to give directions on how the cake you choose is best cut and what kind of knife should be used. Some bakers will supply a knife; you may plan to decorate it with flowers and ribbons. Make a note on your calendar to call the baker and confirm all details a few days before the wedding.

Your choice is not limited to the traditional light-colored cake with three tiers. You may have as many tiers or layers as you wish and you may choose any flavor. Take into consideration the season and location of your wedding; if you are having an outdoor affair or a reception during the warmer months, do not order a cream filling that could easily spoil. You might opt for a cake that is traditionally served in a foreign country. French profiteroles are small puff pastries filled with cream that are stacked in a pyramid shape. German chocolate cake is a milk-chocolate cake with a coconut cream icing. Viennese cakes are rich, deep chocolate confections. Italian rum cake is a white cake with thick, creamy icing between the layers, generously laced with liquor. Perhaps you would prefer a carrot cake, or a banana bread, or even an old-fashioned Americana angel food cake. The choice is completely your own. The secret is in the visual presentation and in making certain that this delicious dessert is large enough to serve all of your guests.

A tiered wedding cake may be decorated in many different styles; it can be completely covered with flowers or each tier may have a border of colored trim. The top of the cake may include the traditional bride-and-groom statuette or you may choose to use real flowers in a small glass. Check whether your baker or your florist will supply these flowers. The top tier of the wedding cake may be made of fruitcake and is usually kept and frozen by the bride and groom for their first anniversary. There are variations upon this tradition; the top tier may serve as the groom's cake, which would be cut into small pieces and boxed separately for the guests to take as souvenirs. The groom's cake is often a separate cake entirely, either fruit or pound, and tradition holds that a single woman who places this cake under her pillow will dream of the man she will marry. The groom's cake is not obligatory.

For large receptions, two cakes are often linked with small plastic bridges or Victorian-style gates; some elaborate cakes include little water fountains and ice sulptures! A multitiered cake is usually assembled at the reception site rather than delivered in one piece, so make arrangements for the time needed to do so. The cake-cutting ceremony takes place approximately one hour before the bride and groom will leave to change into their going-away clothes. If you are having an orchestra and a master of ceremonies, an announcement will be made to bring your guest's attention to the cake cutting. The groom places his right hand over the bride's hand, and together they make the first cut in the bottom tier. They divide this slice and eat it; it's always fun to feed each other the first bite. The rest of the cake should be cut and served by a person to whom this task has been designated in advance. If you have made your own cake for an at-home reception, have a damp cloth handy so the person cutting the cake can clean the knife from time to time. Don't forget to have your photographer snap a photo of your cake, because if it is as delectable as you plan, once it is cut it will never look the same!

24

# X MARKS THE SPOT— PAPERS YOU'LL SIGN

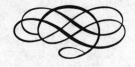

*Xanthe: Hand me my glasses, love. This print gets tinier and tinier as the contract gets longer and longer.*

*Xavier: If you're finished with Page 229A, and addendum B, pass them over here.*

*Both: At least it's in English!*

You and your groom will sign your names many times on everything from binding legal documents to a set of directions for Aunt Nellie to get to the ceremony. The key factor to remember whenever you set your signatures permanently is: Read every item carefully before you sign it. Any agreement should spell out all liabilities and it is easier for all parties to understand if it is in writing. A handshake does not a contract make.

The most important paper you will have to obtain is your marriage license. Every state requires this certificate; it must be completed by your officiator and signed by your witnesses on the day of your wedding. You and your groom must go to your city clerk's office with the following items: a doctor's certificate verifying the results of necessary blood tests and physical examinations, proof of citizenship, and proof of age or your parents' consent to marry. It will take a waiting period of two to three days to get your marriage license, and it is usually valid for thirty days. The groom traditionally pays the fee for the marriage license.

As you make all of the plans for your wedding celebration, make sure that everyone you hire and all services you wish rendered are contracted in writing. Check that every financial obligation is noted. Before you sign the contracts, be clear about your liability should you find it necessary to cancel the contract. Your State Attorney's office or your own lawyer will be able to supply you with any information you need; laws regulating fees for contract cancellation do vary from one state to another.

Here is a list that will outline some of the many contracts and receipts you must get in writing before your wedding. Make certain that all financial estimates and delivery dates and times are specified. Even if the quantity of papers weighs as much as your wedding cake, it is the only way to guarantee protection for both you—the consumer—and all of the vendors you will hire.

*1. Your receipt for bridal wear—all rental agreements for tuxedos and all delivery dates and alteration requirements for your ensemble and your attendants' dresses.*

*2. Your catering contract for the reception.*

*3. Your contract for all floral requirements.*

*4. Your agreement with your travel agent for your honeymoon—check all airline tickets, hotel reservation slips, visas, passports, ground-transportation reservations, and a full itinerary list.*

*5. The receipts for jewelry purchases—check that all details including weight, quality, engraving charges, and delivery dates are listed.*

*6. Your limousine-service rental—list all directions, addresses and times of pick up.*

*7. Your contract with musicians.*

*8. Your contract for photography.*

*9. Your agreement with your printer for all invitations, announcements, enclosure cards, informal notes, and other paper products.*

*10. Your reservation and contract for your reception —location and services.*

*11. Your agreement with your baker for the wedding cake.*

If there is any item that seems to be missing from a contract, no matter how small, have it written in by the person with whom you are doing business.

A marriage contract is something to consider if you and your groom wish to define or express differently any right in your marriage that is customarily taken for granted. If you have any specific obligations or duties which you feel must be added to your formal commitment of marriage, or if there are certain legal or social constrictions which you mutually agree to delete from your personal marriage declaration, you may choose to put these in writing in a formal marriage contract. As cold hearted and unromantic as this may sound, a marriage contract can serve as the departure point for a happier and healthier day-to-day living situation. If it is grounded in love, or concern for mutual understanding, a marriage contract may be the reaffirmation that will lead to clarity and respect on the part of both the bride and groom. Even those couples who do not think of their marriages as contractual in nature have built up a nonverbal contract over their years together, and if two people decide that they would rather make this pledge in writing, they should do so.

Marriage contracts usually cover financial situations, especially when inherited wealth on one party's part is involved. The contract might also include agreements regarding careers, children, adoption, common property, rights if divorce should occur, and the roles and duties that each partner will assume. A marriage contract can solve a problem or relieve stress that might have festered if it had not been articulated in a formal manner. If a marriage contract will solidify a relationship by providing a focus on situations that must be agreed upon prior to the taking of marriage vows, it serves a valuable purpose.

Today's society moves at an incredible pace. If you and your groom feel that a written contract will help you keep time with this world's frantic and often hasty developments, don't let anyone stop you. It is a private affair that may be dealt with by the two of you. If you choose to make it legally binding, your counselor-at-law is the only other person who need be advised of your decision.

One of the more comforting facts in this world of signing and sealing is that you and your groom are in it together. You will have each other's trust and good judgment to rely upon, and what one person might miss when examining a contract, the other will probably notice. You have double protection because two sound minds are involved. Take your time—don't panic, don't rush—so every agreement —from a simple letter describing your seating plan at the reception to a lengthy contract for purchasing a home, will work to your benefit.

## 25
# YEARS TO COME

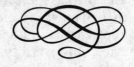

*Yvette: My last name is Smith.*

*Yardley: My last name is Smith.*

*Both: That solves that!*

Amidst all the planning for your wedding, don't forget the day after. That day turns into months and the months into years. Your marriage, along with being a pronouncement of your new commitment, is the first of a number of changes in status that will affect you and your husband's lives publicly. By addressing these issues and planning their implementation before "the day after" your wedding, you will make the smoothest possible transition from single to married life.

Today's society no longer presumes that you will replace your surname with your husband's last name. It is perfectly acceptable to do so, but it is also correct for a woman to keep her own last name. Many women find that for their own business purposes it is much easier to retain the same name they have been using, a name their business associates recognize. Or it may be a name they just happen to like, one that is simply their own, an identity which has been established and accepted. Some women are joining their last name with that of their husband's, hyphenating the two. A third available option is the use of the hyphenated last names by both the husband and the wife. Still a fourth choice is the use of a woman's maiden name as her middle name, then followed by her husband's surname. Whatever you decide, choose one name that you will use for all purposes after your wedding. If you will be using a different name, make arrangements to change all your legal and business documents. These include Social Security registration, driver's license, passport, bank accounts, and charge plates. By making these changes on all your forms of identification, you will have achieved legal acceptance. Nevertheless, if there is any reason whatsoever (complicated legal matters or intricate business proceedings) to change your name formally, do so in court through the proper judicial channels. If you have chosen any other name than the traditional, it is helpful to include a small printed card in your invitations and announcements. The card may read:

*Jane Burton and Mark Geller*
*wish to announce that both*
*will be retaining their present names*
*for all legal and social purposes*
*after their marriage*
*May 24, 1980*

or:

> *After their marriage on May 24, 1980*
> *Jane and Mark will share the surname Burton-Geller*

or:

> *After marriage,*
> *Jane Burton will assume the surname Burton-Geller*

The days when a marriage meant that two people became one (called by the husband's name), rather than two people sharing one relationship, are gone.

Fortunately, current law requires that new joint loans or credit card accounts be issued in both your name and your husband's name, even if you share the same surname. This law resulted from the Equal Credit Opportunity Act passed by Congress in 1974, and it means that each of you can establish your own credit history, an invaluable—and heretofore unobtainable—tool in the co-signing of mortgages and other large purchases.

If you are planning to have children, you may give them your name, your husband's name, or both names in the hyphenated fashion. There is no legal obligation to give the father's name.

Your own full name is used for your signature after marriage; the only change may be in your last name. Even if you choose to be addressed by your husband's name (Mrs. John L. Jones), you do not sign any legal papers, checks, or correspondence this way. You may place that name under your signature or to the left of it (in parentheses if handwritten, without parentheses if typed), but your actual name writing should include your first name and should not include a title. If you wish to indicate your title (Mrs., Ms., Miss), do so by writing it in parentheses in front of your signature.

As you both meet your new families, your respective in-laws, aunts, uncles, and grandparents, there may be a few awkward moments as you establish how you will address one another. If there is anyone who fails to volunteer this information, don't be shy—use your most diplomatic tone (do so in private if there's any real embarrassment) and simply ask that person what he or she would like to be called.

One of the most intricate issues of your new status will be how you and your groom will plan your budget. Whether you will combine incomes or rely on one person's salary for bill paying, take pencil and paper in hand and do some quick calculations. List all your fixed expenses (rent, food, insurance, phone and utility bills) and your flexible expenses (clothing, entertainment, vacation). Try to include monthly savings in your fixed expenses. Remember that a budget is a plan, a schedule that may be changed, so the skiing trip that you forego this month in order to buy a new washing machine may be included in next month's plan. However, your fixed expenses—those you know in advance and must pay on a monthly, quarterly, or annual basis—must take priority. The guide for rent spending has traditionally been one week's salary or one quarter of your gross income. Read every word of a lease or mortgage plan before you sign it; it is wise for you and your husband to take a copy of the lease home and examine it thoroughly, rather than pressuring yourselves into a quick business transaction in a rental agent's office.

Wedding anniversaries have been celebrated like birthdays, but unlike birthdays, an anniversary may be considered a moveable feast. You might choose to have a big party to warm the cold of winter with celebration even though your actual wedding date is in the early spring. Have fun!

There are traditional gifts to celebrate specific years of anniversaries; the most popular seem to be the first (paper), the fifth (wood), the tenth (tin or aluminum), the twenty-fifth (silver), and the fiftieth (gold). Gifts are often given in the same color rather than the material; yellow roses are sent to represent the gold of a fiftieth-year celebration. Oddly enough, these popular dates coincide with recent statistics that claim these years mark the healthiest and happiest for marriage stability. American divorce rates are lowest at these points; only 4.5 percent of all divorces happen during the first year of marriage, this percentage increases during the second (8.6 percent), third (9.4 percent) and fourth (8.9 percent) years, goes back down in the tenth year, and reaches the all-time low of 1 percent after twenty-five years of marriage. Tradition and fact thereby agree, and can offer everyone a forewarning for those times when some extra expressions of commitment might prove helpful. Even the most blissful marriage will have moments of tension, but if you and your groom pledge to work continually at perfecting your relationship, throughout the years to come, your realistic outlook will guide you to a happier life together.

## 26
# ZOOM LENS

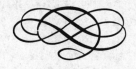

*Zelda: Oh, Zach—please be serious for just one more minute.*

*Zachariah: C'mon, honey—smile! This is our happy day.*

*Both: You already took it?*

This chapter has been saved for last because next to your lives together, photographs last the longest. Even if you just ask a friend to snap some candid shots, you'll regret if you don't make some sort of arrangements for pictures to be taken. There will never be a repeat performance of your wedding, so you'll only have one chance to capture the event on film. The trick to good picture taking is the eye behind the lens, so begin your search for a qualified photographer as soon as you've set your wedding date. The good ones are booked well in advance, especially for the busier wedding months of June, August, September, and December. Ask friends for recommendations; make appointments with various photographers to see their samples. If you've seen a collection of shots you particularly like, track down the specific photographer, not just any member of the staff or studio whose name is printed on the pictures. You may wish to ask for references from the photographer, and be wary if you are only shown one or two samples. An experienced photographer will have a large, well-stocked portfolio. There is an organization called the Professional Photographers of America, of which your photographer is probably a member, which has established a code of ethics specifically for wedding photography.

Your photography contract is one you will want in writing with each and every detail spelled out. Find out all costs, including the prices of various sizes of photos (eight by ten inches, five by seven inches, and three and one-half by five inches are standard sizes, but you may want a larger portrait or smaller wallet photos; some couples use a picture in a folder card for thank-you notes) and albums. Ask how many photographs you will be obligated to buy. Make sure that you agree on an actual date of delivery of the finished work and that you know exactly what type of pictures (color, black and white, double exposure, special effect, vignette, full-length, close-up) you will receive. Discuss in advance and list in your contract all the locations in which you will want the photographer to shoot and the exact time you will need the photographer at each place. You may want to have pictures taken at home before the ceremony, at the church, at the reception; perhaps you'll want your formal portrait taken in a nearby park or woodland. Give the photographer maps if necessary. If he wishes to see the locations before the actual wedding day (usually for lighting and filter requirements), make arrangements for this; it is certainly to your benefit. (There should not be an additional charge for this, however). Also, mention that you may request special pictures; make sure your photographer agrees to this. Ask about the photographer's filing system and how long negatives are kept, in case you decide to have prints made some years later. Once you have discussed every detail with your photographer, make a firm financial agreement on the total for all charges, from deposit to final payment. Some photographers use standardized contracts; read the fine print before signing.

The two types of wedding photographs are formal and candid. Formal portraits are posed, while candid photographs are shot spontaneously without the subject being posed. A formal, full-length portrait of you in your wedding ensemble may be taken several weeks in advance of your wedding date, especially if it is of importance to you to have your photograph published in newspapers. Most journals require that a glossy photo be submitted one to two weeks prior to the publication date, which is usually the day after or closest Sunday to the wedding date. This portrait can be shot in the location of your choice, but is usually taken at the photographer's studio or the bridal shop where you've purchased your dress. Remember to take all the accessories that you will wear on your wedding day with you to the shooting. This includes everything from lingerie and shoes to jewelry and makeup. Photographers will usually supply a substitute or dummy bouquet for the portrait, so a description of the flowers you'll carry will be necessary. You may opt to hold a prayer book or a single flower for your portrait; this is perfectly acceptable and you will be able to choose the book or guarantee the flower's freshness. You must decide if you want your portrait to be color or black and white, and you should know how many prints you will want to purchase. Remember parents, family, newspapers, and your own needs when taking your count.

There are definite benefits to having your portrait taken on your actual wedding day. You will not have to transport your gown and accessories to a studio, your flowers will be your own, and the excitement and bouyancy of your wedding day will be written on your face and captured in your expression. There is great truth in the old adage that all brides are beautiful, but practically speaking, they are at their loveliest on their wedding day. Formal portraits of you and your groom and with your families should be taken after your guests have gone through the receiving line if your reception is scheduled to immediately follow the ceremony. Your guests should not have to wait for the festivities to begin while formal pictures are being taken. Since going through the receiving line is the first activity for guests at the reception, you can plan to greet them in the line and let them move on to sipping champagne while you have your pictures taken. This will also alleviate the problem of the impatient guest who doesn't care to wait and might amuse himself by distracting you and your groom during the formal picture taking. As treasured as your guests and friends may be, formal photographs are taken far more speedily without interruption.

Your makeup for your wedding is very important for your photographs. You will want to wear makeup that will be comfortable for the entire day (you will have chances to touch up, but even a touch-up shouldn't take any great amount of time). Your wedding portrait and all your wedding photographs should be natural, not strained, and so should your makeup. Use a liquid or cream foundation rather than a matte finish, which tends to dull natural highlights. Do not overdo with blusher, as it will show black in a black and white photo. Medium shades of lipstick read best, and do be generous with lip gloss. Heavy eye makeup is not necessary, mascara definitely is.

As valuable as your formal portraits will be, the candid photos may be the ones you'll look at and share with friends more often. They are the random, casual shots that record a smile, a dance, a conversation, even a private moment that is totally unaffected, one in which the subjects are often unaware that they are being photographed. You may find a photographer whose portrait work you like, but whose candid style is not suitable to your needs. You may arrange for these areas to be handled separately and engage the services of two photographers. If you have certain persons whom you definitely want included in the pictures of your wedding, ask a close friend to point these people out and introduce that friend to the photographer before the festivities begin.

If friends and relatives wish to bring their pocket cameras along, permit them to do so. In fact, it is often wise to encourage this, since friends know other friends personally and may snap a photo of a special moment that no one else sees. These home photos are also good fun because they are usually very casual and are not expected to be works of art. If you choose to have a friend do the official photography, you should pay for all film, developing, and reproduction costs. Giving a small gift of thanks to this friend for the time and talent involved is a nice gesture.

Because photographs are such lasting mementos, make sure that the pictures—especially your formal portraits—reflect your personality and the mood that you want set for your wedding. When you look back at your album a year later, you want to recognize everyone pictured, including yourself! If you feel that the photographer is forcing you into a pose that is totally uncomfortable for you and your groom, if you have no desire to purchase a photo of each of your left hands newly adorned with rings, or if Aunt Nellie just refuses to smile, speak up. Your discussions with the photographer before the wedding should keep problems to a minimum, if they exist at all, and a good photographer is used to dealing with the nervousness and tension that is often present on wedding days. An experienced photographer will also go unnoticed, becoming almost invisible but still totally available at your ceremony and reception. He should inconspicuously capture the candid shots and quickly and efficiently organize the formal portraits. Pictures are taken of the wedding—the wedding is not taking place for the image maker.

If you decide that you want a collection of close-ups or a videotape of your wedding, the options are yours; modern photography and filmmaking can offer you a range of possibilities that becomes greater as technology advances. Your wedding is a happy time involving special people that *can* be permanently recorded. If a picture says a thousand words, a good photographer should be able to produce a novel of epic proportions about your wedding.

# IN CONCLUSION

May your wedding planning be as easy as A, B, C, and your marriage as timeless as all communication.

# INDEX